René

MAGRITTE

by James Thrall Soby

THE MUSEUM OF MODERN ART, NEW YORK

in collaboration with

the Rose Art Museum, Brandeis University;

The Art Institute of Chicago;

The Pasadena Art Museum

and the University Art Museum, University of California, Berkeley

Distributed by Doubleday & Company, Garden City, New York

© The Museum of Modern Art, 1965
11 West 53 Street, New York, N. Y. 10019
Library of Congress Catalogue Card
Number 65–28610
Designed by Joseph Bourke DelValle.
Printed in the U. S. A.
by Kingsport Press, Inc.
Second Printing

CONTENTS

ACKNOWLEDGMENTS

ON BEHALF OF the Trustees of the Museum of Modern Art, and of the Rose Art Museum, Brandeis University, The Art Institute of Chicago, The Pasadena Art Museum, and the University Art Museum, Berkeley, we wish to express our gratitude to those whose cooperation has made this exhibition possible. René Magritte has shown keen interest in both the exhibition and the catalogue, and has responded graciously to our frequent questions. The sponsorship of the Belgian Government has enabled us to include essential works from European collections. Besides arranging this support, Emile Langui, Administrateur Général, and Jan van Lerberghe, Conseiller, Ministère de l'Education Nationale et de la Culture, also gave warm and essential cooperation in locating works and arranging meetings with collectors, as did Robert Giron, Directeur, Société Auxiliaire des Expositions du Palais des Beaux-Arts, Brussels.

Several friends and associates of Magritte gave advice and assistance that contributed greatly to the success of the exhibition: Harry Torczyner, who from the beginning of our work to its completion, put his intimate knowledge of Magritte's work at our disposal; E. L. T. Mesens, one of the first to recognize Magritte's importance; Patrick Waldberg, author of a forthcoming book on Magritte, and its editor, P. G. van Hecke; Alexander Iolas, Magritte's dealer in New York, Paris and Geneva. For advice and assistance we also called on William N. Copley and Jean de Menil. Unpublished material used in the text of the catalogue was contributed by the artist, Claude Spaak and George Melly. For editorial assistance in the preparation of the text, thanks are hereby expressed to Alfred H. Barr, Jr., Françoise Boas, Jennifer Licht, Alicia Legg, Margaret Scolari and Melissa Soby.

WILLIAM C. SEITZ,
Curator, Department of Painting and Sculpture Exhibitions

JAMES THRALL SOBY,
Co-Director of the Exhibition

THE DIFFERENCES in cultural heritage between the Flemings and the Walloons are complicated and require more extended study than is possible here. For our purpose it is perhaps enough to note that René Magritte, born and raised in the Walloon country, was more susceptible to French influence than his Flemish colleagues, a fact which may help explain his early embrace of the surrealist movement centering in Paris. He was born in 1898 in the town of Lessines, in the province of Hainaut, halfway between Charleroi and the North Sea. His childhood was spent there, in Gilly, in Châtelet and in Charleroi.

Magritte was twenty before he moved with his family to Brussels, where he has lived ever since, except for three years in Paris during the late 1920s and occasional trips. To those who have been puzzled by his preference for bourgeois surroundings and the most conventional possible way of life, an answer has been given by George Melly, who says of Magritte: "He is a secret agent, his object is to bring into disrepute the whole apparatus of bourgeois reality. Like all saboteurs, he avoids detection by dressing and behaving like everybody else."[1] To this statement an American footnote might be added. Magritte works in a sense like an Indian. He backtracks, swerves, disguises his footprints—and moves steadily forward in the silent forest which shelters all true creative activity. As a result, it has been impossible to trace his career in the strict chronological sequence that comforts art historians and critics.

As in the case of many artists and less talented mortals, the memory of childhood vacations has been of lasting importance to Magritte's consciousness. One thinks of his associate in surrealism, Yves Tanguy, who all his life drew inspiration from his boyhood memories of the summertime Brittany coast, with its menhirs brooding in the fields and the stones of the beaches tumbling polished and helpless in the tides.

As a youth Magritte went often to the old cemetery at Soignies. The cemetery's granite monuments and the wooden caskets in its crypt have played a recurrent role in his art's iconography (pages 46, 47).[2] His mother drowned herself in the Sambre River when he was only fourteen. The tragic event may have given his sensitive mind a sombre cast, reflected only very occasionally in pictures whose wit seems mordant as well as playful.

During adolescence Magritte became interested in painting and for several years studied its history and practice at the Academy of Fine Arts in Brussels. But the most important single event of his career occurred in 1922.

[1] George Melly, author of BBC Monitor Film, 1965, London. (Bibl. 140)

[2] It is more than possible that Magritte had also known Antoine Wiertz's picture, *Precipitate Burial* (1854) (opposite), in which coffins are upended in a fantastic manner. The parallel was first suggested by John Canaday in "Floating Rocks and Flaming Tubas," *Horizon*, Jan., 1962. (Bibl. 38)

Antoine Wiertz: *Precipitate Burial.* 1854. Oil, 71 x 100″. Musée Wiertz, Brussels

In that year a lifelong friend, Marcel Lecomte, whose likeness in stone appears in *Memory of a Voyage* (page 53), showed him a reproduction of Giorgio de Chirico's 1914 painting, *The Song of Love* (opposite). The picture's impact on young Magritte was overwhelming. Indeed, according to his own account, it moved him to tears.[3]

Magritte's reaction to de Chirico's haunting dislocations of reality was by no means unique. Both André Breton, surrealism's founder, and Yves Tanguy, one of the movement's most dedicated adherents, at separate intervals saw a comparable "metaphysical" de Chirico in a gallery window while riding on a Paris bus. Both men jumped off the bus and examined the picture with an excitement never to subside for either of them. In this connection Magritte's own words are most relevant: "It was in fact in 1922 when I first came to know the works of Chirico. A friend then showed me a reproduction of his painting, *The Song of Love*, which I always consider to be a work by the greatest painter of our time in the sense that it deals with poetry's ascendancy over painting and the various manners of painting. Chirico was the first to dream of *what must be painted* and not *how to paint*." [4]

About five years later Magritte saw two books of poems by Paul Eluard, illustrated by Max Ernst's superb collages. The books were *Répétitions* and *Les Malheurs des Immortels*. Of the first named book (illustration opposite), Magritte has written: "In illustrating *Répétitions* by Paul Eluard, Max Ernst has demonstrated magnificently that through collages obtained from old magazine illustrations, one could easily surpass everything which gives traditional painting its prestige . . ." [5] The two Eluard-Ernst books sometimes furnish close parallels of imaginative climate with Magritte's own art and we know from many first-hand accounts that Ernst, like de Chirico, was a guardian angel—or devil—of Magritte's early years as a painter.

Around 1915, long before his exposure to the art of de Chirico and Ernst, Magritte began to think seriously of becoming a professional painter. He says that he then had received an illustrated catalogue of futurist pictures and adds that half seriously and half in jest he "came to know of a new way of painting." [6] He adds: "I cannot doubt that a pure and powerful sentiment, namely

de Chirico: *The Song of Love.* 1914. Oil, 28¾ x 23½″. Private collection, New York

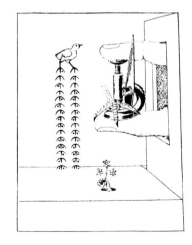

Ernst: Illustration for *Répétitions* by Paul Eluard, Paris, Au Sans Pareil [1922]

[3] René Magritte, "Esquisse Auto-biographique," *L'Oeuvre de René Magritte,* "Editions de la Connaissance," Brussels, 1962, p. 17. (Bibl. 128)
[4] René Magritte, letter to the writer, May 20, 1965.
[5] René Magritte manuscript dated July 1938 of lecture given at Museum of Fine Arts, Antwerp, Nov. 20, 1938. (Bibl. 9)
[6] René Magritte, "Lifeline," *View,* v. 7, no. 2, Dec., 1946, p. 21. (Bibl. 9)

eroticism, saved me from slipping into the traditional chase after formal perfection. My interest lay entirely in provoking an emotional shock." [7] It might be argued, of course, that the futurists' interests were not always dissimilar from his own, at least by comparison with the more purely esthetic preoccupations of the Parisian cubists. Magritte seems not to have known much about cubism until slightly later, possibly because it was easier for Northern Europeans to accept futurism's clamor than it was for the French who, with not altogether justifiable pride, felt that if foreign artists wanted to amount to anything they should move to the French capital at once.

In any case, the influence of futurism and cubism is apparent in Magritte's *Young Girl* of 1922 (opposite). The picture's faceted divisions obviously owe much to the cubist-futurist rebellion. Yet it must also be noted that the *Young Girl* was painted the very year Magritte first came to know de Chirico's early works. Its figure is overlaid with those rigid triangles which de Chirico had kept in mind since he saw the draftsman's instruments on the desk of his father, an engineer for railroad construction. The wings of Magritte's composition suggest the theatrical definitions of exaggerated space which were an earmark of de Chirico's "metaphysical" period (1911–17) and which Magritte was to use consistently throughout his mature career. The *Young Girl* is an inconclusive work, as might be expected of an apprentice painter who edged his way toward profundity rather than abruptly toppled into it. It was to be another four years before Magritte's idiosyncratic personality as an artist would assert itself. It did so in the large *Menaced Assassin* (page 10).

One is always on treacherous ground in giving a precise iconographical reading to the works of an artist whose inspiration so often travels by the subways of the mind. Nevertheless, the script of the *Menaced Assassin* seems relatively clear. A nude woman lies bleeding from the mouth on a sofa in the background. Her murderer calms his nerves by listening to a gramophone, not yet aware that his exit is blocked by three men peering over a grilled window at the rear of the room, while in the foreground his captors await him with bludgeon and net. The triple extension of perspective—from foyer to living room to distant landscape—reflects Magritte's continuing respect for de Chirico's extreme manipulations of space. But the *Menaced Assassin* has its own prophetic overtones. It foretells the somnambulant irrationality of certain figures in sculpture by Giacometti and in paintings by Balthus, whom Magritte is said to admire greatly. There is almost certainly no question of influence involved here, but only a shared rejection of the abstract premise.

Young Girl. 1922. Oil. Collection Léonce Rigot, Brussels. (Not in exhibition)

[7] "Lifeline," *op. cit.*, p. 21.

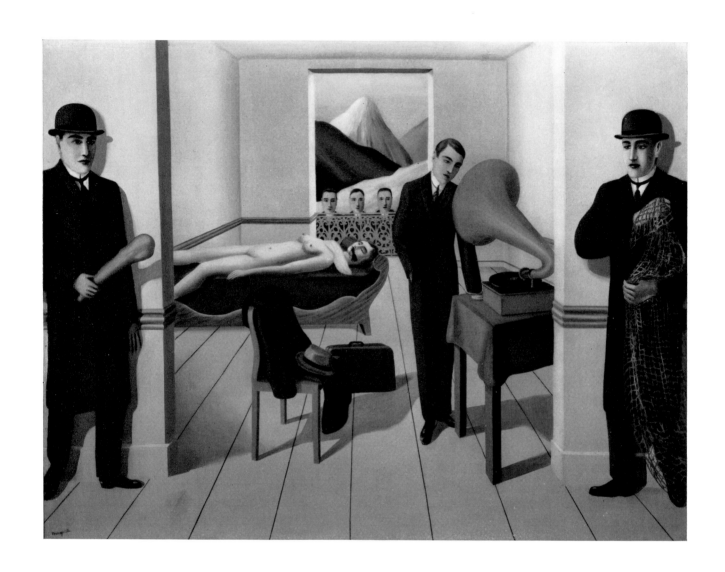

The Menaced Assassin. 1926. Oil, 59⅞ x 76⅞″. Collection E. L. T. Mesens, London

The *Dawn at Cayenne* (opposite), also of 1926, is a far less personal work than the *Assassin*. It shows a wry assembly of unrelated objects on a fluted tableland and its point is too stridently expressed, as often happens when artists and others are converted to a new faith, as Magritte had been in joining the surrealists. It evokes comparison with Tanguy's so-called "African" period of a few years later. But there is this important difference: the deliberate realism of Magritte's image, with its upflung hands, candle, folder and weightless tree, is far from Tanguy's illusory preoccupation with dolmens and stones.

For Magritte's purpose careful, even glossy definition of his subjects was more crucial than the tonal subtleties that Tanguy loved. He was after all the heir, not to the tasteful French fantasists of earlier centuries and to Chardin, but to the Low Countries' occasional berserk demonology in art. Perhaps this is why Magritte's hard finish in technical matters has tended to obscure his accompanying sensitivity and deftness. He has frequently disclaimed any interest in *matière* for its own sake, though there was a brief and on the whole unsuccessful period in the early 1940s when he was seduced by impressionism's outer charms. Perhaps more consistently than any other painter of his generation he has sought what Guillaume Apollinaire called art's greatest potential—surprise. Magritte tells jokes and invents puns in a quiet voice. Many of us listen with avid attention and our number is growing.

The *Man with Newspaper* (page 22) must be one of the earliest of Magritte's pictures of compartmented scenes which are identical in subject except for the fading away of the principal detail—in this case the man reading, who dominates the first frame of the cinema and thereafter is gone, leaving his surroundings intact. And leaving the observer with a sense of unease. It could be that Magritte's choice of a man with newspaper as a subject stems, however obliquely, from André Derain's early (1914) image of the same subject, the *Chevalier X*, now in the Hermitage at Leningrad (opposite). Magritte respectfully included Derain's picture in a list of such more obvious ancestors of his own art as de Chirico, Max Ernst, Picasso and Marcel Duchamp. He referred to "certain works of Derain, *The Man with a Newspaper*, among others, in which an actual newspaper is pasted to the hand of a person." [8] The historical fact seems to be that Derain did at first affix the newspaper to his canvas but later replaced it with a painted replica. The picture was, however, widely reproduced in its collage state. Magritte's *Man with Newspaper* tells its curious story without subtitles. In other pictures such as *The Key of Dreams* (page 24), however, objects are compartmented and in-

Dawn at Cayenne. 1926. Oil, 39⅜ x 28¾". Collection J. Berthold Urvater, Brussels. (Not in exhibition)

Derain: *Chevalier X*. 1914. Oil and pasted paper. (Early stage of painting in Hermitage Museum, Leningrad)

[8] René Magritte, July, 1938, *op. cit.* (Bibl. 9)

scribed with totally irrelevant descriptive names, as if in defiance of the identi-fying logic of the pictures in illustrated children's spelling books. This defiance reaches its most condensed statement in a realistic picture of a pipe inscribed, "This is Not a Pipe" (page 24).[9] Magritte often flaunts reality by giving it its most acceptable guise and then denying it by the old disclaimer, "I never said any such thing."

The unusually macabre *Bold Sleeper* (page 23) supplies in its lower sec-tion a sort of agenda for future iconographical motifs in Magritte's art—a lady's elegant mirror, a bird, a derby hat, a bow, a candle, an apple. And then he turns with poetic skill to that refutation of gravity's powers which has always fascinated him, as though his mind was in orbit long before the age of the spacemen, who today unsupported skip rope in the firmament.

Threatening Weather (page 26) combines a svelte female torso with the ungainly contortions of a tuba and gives her a sturdy wicker chair on which she may rest. These are phantoms, aloft in fog over a placid bay. The picture's luminosity of sky and mist should be answer indeed to those who challenge Magritte's technical gifts because he underplays them. The *Flowers of the Abyss, I* (page 25) is one of many paintings of which the artist himself has given an eloquent description—"The iron bells hanging from the necks of our splendid horses I caused to sprout like dangerous plants from the edge of a chasm."[10] Such bells are, of course, ubiquitous throughout much of the civi-lized world. They hang from the harness of carriages and sleighs. They dangle from infants' cradles and are waved aloft on carnival wands. Perhaps they are a humble rejoinder to the great bells of the cathedrals and churches and their purpose the same—to provide solace against the diurnal stillness.

The False Mirror (page 25) was also painted in 1928 and is an image which in transformed shape and identity is now familiar to millions of people as the trademark of CBS's television programs. The following year Magritte gave a predominant role to paper cut-outs, such as children are taught to unfold to create a startling and recognizable reality of figure or object. Concurrently Magritte made frequent use of tall, cylindrical forms which most readily sug-gest the pawns in a game of chess (pages 44, 45).

The derivation of these forms has long interested the writer. In reply to an inquiry Magritte's close friend, Harry Torczyner, has replied: "The chess-

---

[9] It is amusing to note in this connection what Louis Scutenaire says of the artist: "He smokes endlessly, but only cigarettes—*des noires*. His love of pipes is en-tirely platonic." Louis Scutenaire, *René Magritte*, Brussels, Librairie Sélection, 1947, p. 46, (Bibl. 31)

[10] René Magritte, "Lifeline," *op. cit.*, p. 22.

like figures are transfigurations of what Magritte calls a *bilboquet*, sometimes used in the cup-and-ball game. As Magritte has always been an avid chess player, we get the crossing of a chess figure with a *bilboquet* and the result is a strange creature with wicked snout." [11]

As has already been noted in passing, the exact chronological sequence of Magritte's paintings is often difficult to determine in that he has treated closely related and even identical subjects at separate intervals. Nevertheless, it seems reasonable to assume that the "wicked snout" mentioned by Torczyner is a later invention than the bland, rounded balusters which serve as heads as well as torsos in such paintings as *The Annunciation* (page 30) of 1929. The change in character from knob to spouting nozzle is apparent if we compare *The Annunciation* to *The Rights of Man* (page 44), executed several years later. The artist apparently became fascinated by the shape of a portable welding torch such as plumbers use in repairing small pipes. The indentations in the handles of these tools are designed to be enwrapped by the plumber's fingers; the tools' terminal points do indeed suggest "a wicked snout." It may be that their intense flame has set fire in *The Rights of Man* to a tuba whose convoluted form is not unlike that of plumbing beneath a sink. In *The Ladder of Fire* (page 27), however, a tuba and a chair have been kindled simply by a flaming bundle of paper on the floor. Whatever its source, the blaze was hard to extinguish as an imaginative way of enlivening contours. It soon spread to the gawky necks of Salvador Dali's giraffes.[12]

In the wonderfully lyric and sensual *Elemental Cosmogony* (page 45) the blow-torch snout spews flame into a sky whose clouds envelop the cubic structures, like children's building blocks, dear to Magritte. The mannequin body to which the snout is attached holds aloft a leaf—another recurrent iconographical detail in this painter's art. At the lower right reappears the by now familiar bell, this time used more as an anchor to the composition than as a decorative accessory. Magritte's periodic absorption in dividing a given composition into self-contained compartments has been noted. Perhaps this interest in shuffling and reassembling pictorial themes stemmed originally from his youthful admiration for de Chirico, who often painted pictures complete within the picture, preserving intact the identity of such sub-images, whereas masters like Holbein had made them half-disguised components of the total effect, as in his famous *The Ambassadors*. At any rate, in *On the Threshold of Liberty* (page 23) and numerous other works Magritte divides his imagina-

[11] Harry Torczyner, letter to the writer, July 6, 1965.
[12] For a comment on Magritte's preoccupation with fire, cf., "René Magritte ou la révélation objective." *Les Beaux-Arts*, Brussels, no. 203, May 1, 1936, p. 19. (Bibl. 59)

tive process into segments, so to speak, which he then puts together again, their weird concourse this time ordained by an antiquated cannon.

Magritte also dismembered female anatomy in the *Eternal Evidence* and several other works (page 32). It may be far-fetched to say that he did so in oblique tribute to Manet and yet Manet's art seems to have haunted him, as will appear in his paraphrase of the French master's *The Balcony* (page 46). About the renowned *Olympia* Magritte had this to say: "They wished to destroy Manet's *Olympia* and the critics reproached that painter for showing women cut into fragments, because the only thing he showed of a woman placed behind a wardrobe was the top part of her body, the lower part being hidden by the wardrobe."[13] Magritte's reading of the celebrated Manet picture is subjective, to put it mildly, since its model's body is bisected but in no way concealed by the wardrobe, which is in the background.[14]

Of *The Human Condition, I* (page 35) Magritte has written a quite literal description: "The problem of the window led to *La Condition humaine*. In front of a window, as seen from the interior of a room, I placed a picture that represented precisely the portion of landscape blotted out by the picture. For instance, the tree represented in the picture displaced the tree situated behind it, outside the room. For the spectator it was simultaneously inside the room; in the picture, and outside, in the real landscape, in thought. Which is how we see the world, namely, outside of us, though having only one representation of it within us."[15] The basic concept of *The Human Condition* was transcribed from landscape to seascape in a second version of the theme (opposite), and this time the easel shares the foreground with an old cannon ball, perhaps intended as a reminder of warfare's simpler glories in the past. Like de Chirico before him, Magritte is fond of temporal cross-references and of the ambiguity between indoor and outdoor settings which a window can evoke. The fusion of painted with actual landscape is again utilized in the exceptionally lyric little *Fair Captive, II* (page 35). The same sleight-of-hand approach was revived years later by Magritte in *The Promenades of Euclid* (page 34), though now the subject is a cityscape which in precision of detailed vistas recalls early Flemish masters like Roger van der Weyden.

Two of Magritte's images which cling to memory with fierce tenacity were painted in the mid-1930s—*The Red Model* and *Portrait* (page 38, frontis-

Manet: *Olympia*. 1863. Oil, 51¼ x 74¾″. The Louvre, Paris

The Human Condition, II. 1935. Oil, 39⅜ x 28¾″. Collection Mme Happé-Lorge, Brussels. (Not in exhibition)

[13] René Magritte, July, 1938, *op. cit.* (Bibl. 9)

[14] Magritte also reassorted a nude woman's body in a widely reproduced picture, *The Rape*, in which he converts to pictorial terms Percy Bysshe Shelley's traumatic vision of Mary Shelley's breasts turning into eyes, a vision which sent Shelley screaming from their room.

[15] "Lifeline," *op. cit.*, p. 22.

piece). Both exist in different scales and media and both are particularly successful rejections of everyday reality. In one, shoes inexplicably sprout human toes; it "shouts a cry of alarm," as has been said.[16] In the other, an open eye in the middle of a ham steak replaces the marrow bone to frighten the person about to eat the meat. In both pictures, as often happens in Magritte's art, a single contradictory detail challenges our visual habits. For example, of the many people who have seen the *Portrait* nearly all insist that the eye replaces a fried egg. There is no egg in the picture. Similarly, those of us who have worked on this exhibition and book disagree among ourselves as to whether the gigantic boulder in *The Glass Key* (page 57) clings precariously to a mountain side or has already fallen into space. In viewing Magritte's paintings it is always well to remember that everything seems proper. And then abruptly the rape of commonsense occurs, usually in broad daylight.

The projection of obsessive iconographical elements into new surroundings and combinations is typical of Magritte's procedure. Thus the human feet in workmen's boots in the *Red Model* thrust out again from ladies' high-heeled pumps in "*Philosophy in the Boudoir*" (page 39). In the latter picture a woman's nipples stare out of their translucent peignoir to suggest both anger and the quite different emotion aroused by the murmur of breasts under summer silk. But Magritte is also capable of shifting emphasis to new pictorial inventions. He did so in the well-known *Therapeutic* (page 42), his stomach aflutter with birds, his hat clapped on a head without neck, his absurd cloak, his hopelessly ponderous traveling bag and his cane bent into unlikely shadow.

Even though, as already claimed, exact chronological discussion of Magritte's painting is almost impossible, perhaps this is the place to say that during the war years of 1940–45 Magritte decided to try his hand occasionally at painting in the manner of the French impressionists, especially Renoir. The result was not happy and Magritte's work in the impressionist vein was so badly received by friends and foes alike that he called it, half defiantly, "accursed." [17]

His obeisance to nature over, Magritte quickly returned to his own instinctive technique. In 1949 he painted a beguiling paraphrase of Manet's

[16] *Les Beaux-Arts*, Brussels, *op. cit.* (Bibl. 59)

[17] Louis Scutenaire, *René Magritte*, Ministry of Education, Brussels, 1964, pp. 12–13. (Bibl. 32)

The word "accursed" does not apply, as is often thought, to what Magritte has called "L'époque vache." The latter phrase applies only to a period of months in 1948 when Magritte was assembling rather hastily an exhibition of his paintings to be held in Paris, where his name was beginning to be forgotten, except among the *aficionados*, due to the isolation imposed by the war.

Balcony (page 46), thus reaffirming his somewhat incongruous interest in the French master. Magritte has retained such details of Manet's picture as the potted plant at the left, the railing in front and the shutters which frame the French artist's eminently respectable figures. But he has converted the figures themselves into caskets, remembered from boyhood visits to the old crypts in the cemetery at Soignies. A fourth casket lurks in the dark background to replace the servant with a samovar in Manet's image of high bourgeois affluence. The silver handles and coffin nails supply the highlights given off by metallic objects in the interior of Manet's picture.

The metamorphosis of sacrosanct into surrealist imagery is less extensive when Magritte turns to David's celebrated portrait of Madame Récamier (page 47). It could be that he found the neo-Spartanism of David's temperament, before the latter was seduced by the glory of painting both an Emperor and a Pope, less congenial (except in technique) than Manet's unrelenting worldliness. At any rate, he replaces Madame Récamier's figure with a casket but otherwise does little mischief to accessory details. He retains the quite hideous lamp in David's picture and also the stool beneath Madame's chaise longue and her gown overflowing to the floor. It could be that the decorative style of the First Empire, in good part David's invention, was less susceptible to fantasy's embroidery than that of the Third Empire under which Manet came to maturity.

Magritte, like Ernst, has always had an obsessive interest in birds. He paints doves, one of them inside and the other inexplicably outside the ribcage of a man (page 42). He paints a solemn conclave of owls, rehearsing their wisdom and indignant at daylight's intrusion (page 60). Even more often he paints eagles. They crown cemetery monuments with their vast wings in *Fortune Made* (page 17). He allows them their own flesh in *The Fanatics* (page 61), but then in *The Idol* (page 68) sends another kind of bird aloft calcified, flying majestic and high and perhaps gazing below to see Icarus floundering in his reverse doom. Not even the blazing fire in *The Stated Place* can thaw the stone eagle's blood, and the eagle's wings become mountain peaks (page 61).[18]

Magritte applies the process of calcification to subjects other than birds, as though the granite monuments at Soignies were still much in mind. In *Memory of a Voyage, III* (page 52) he creates a stone still life and projects it against

Manet: *The Balcony*. 1869. Oil, 67¾ x 49¼". The Louvre, Paris

David: *Portrait of Madame Julie Récamier.* 1800. Oil, 68⅛ x 96". The Louvre, Paris

[18] In painting this picture Magritte has acknowledged his debt to Edgar Allan Poe, who dreamed of "an immense mountain which assumes exactly the form of a bird with wings spread." "René Magritte, La Ligne de Vie," *Combat* 3, no. 105, Dec. 10, 1938. (Bibl. 9)

a rocky cleft. In *Intimate Journal* (page 53) a calcified man looks for a speck in his companion's eye and both figures share the pock-marked surface of the boulders amid which they stand. *The Lovers* (page 56) portrays a man and woman who breathe with the gills and mouths of fish, while beyond them a sailing vessel takes the place of the concrete-block horizons in other works by Magritte. This image is notable for its impudent breaches of plausibility.

In 1953 a series of eight murals, known collectively as *The Enchanted Domain*, was unveiled by the Communal Casino at Knokke-Le Zoute which had commissioned them. The actual murals were executed by Raymond Art and his assistants in the grand salon of the casino, after oil studies by Magritte.

Meanwhile Magritte's calcified subjects continued to appear. In the version of *The Memory of a Voyage* painted in 1955 (page 53), Magritte's friend Marcel Lecomte, as briefly noted, appears quite literally petrified in his Chesterfield coat. Beside him lies the Androclean lion that often appears in Magritte's later works (page 48). It would be tempting to see the lion as a symbol of reformed ferocity except that the artist has repeatedly disclaimed any interest in symbolism. "Sometimes I hate symbols," he once confessed to a *Time Magazine* reporter.[19] He wishes his paintings to say what they say and nothing more. Magritte's art is essentially direct rather than allusive and this is its hypnotic charm. The observer shakes his head in disbelief and then accepts with pride, like a moose balancing the candelabra of new antlers sprouting from its head. Magritte's passion for rock formations is again evident in two remarkable works. *The Invisible World* and *The Glass Key* (pages 54, 57). In the first the ubiquitous boulder perches on a balcony; in the second it looms at the summit of a gorge. Between them the two pictures define the extremes of Magritte's imaginative range: panoramas and the enclosed space of small rooms. Very often his objects are set free in the firmament or jammed within impossibly narrow chambers. He uses space to heighten his art's ambiguity, just as he contrasts—and often deliberately confuses—buoyancy and dead weight, as when a medieval castle rises above the sea on ramparts which logically should sink rather than sustain it (page 55). Magritte inherits the ancient belief that magic is explicable only when it is utterly inexplicable. And Magritte himself is a magician of the very first order.

All the artist's close friends agree that he is constantly preoccupied with color. This is a fact which the surface blandness of his technique conceals from the casual observer but it is obvious on careful scrutiny if still deliberately startling and puzzling. As early as 1928 in *Threatening Weather* (page 26) he used subtle blends of tone and light to define the odd medley of objects emerg-

Fortune Made. 1957. Oil, 23½ x 19¾". Zwirner Gallery, Cologne. (Not in exhibition)

[19] *Time*, June 21, 1948.

ing from the fog. In *Perpetual Motion* (page 31) the reflections of objects in a tiny pool are masterly in the sense that the fifteenth century Flemish painters would have understood the word.

Much later Magritte's regard for luxury of pigment and color became more pronounced, as in *"The Tomb of the Wrestlers"* with its seductive reds (color plate) and the *Listening Chamber* (page 41) in beautifully perfidious green. Both pictures are among the most memorable of Magritte's career. The rose's petals and the apple's stem press against the ceiling in rooms which seem like storage bins in the dwarfs' suite in the Reggia dei Gonzaga at Mantua. The walls reflect with astonishing richness the red of the flower and the green of the fruit. The daylight from the window gives the objects a superb roundness of form, as in stereoptic slides of the finest quality.

Mention has already been made of three kinds of metamorphosis which recur in Magritte's art: interior to exterior setting; deep to shallow perspective; dead weight to buoyancy. A fourth should be added. Around 1950 Magritte began to paint street scenes in which houses and pavements are plunged into a darkness relieved only by artificial lights. But the sky above blazes in the noon sun or is illuminated by stars and the moon to create an incredible brightness. Magritte himself has had this to say on the subject: "An inspired thought which resembles the visible thing offered to it becomes what was offered to it and evokes its mystery. An inspired thought combines what is offered to it *in an order evocative of mystery*. For example: it combines a nocturnal landscape and a starry sky (my picture 'The Empire of Light'). A thought limited to similarities can only contemplate a starry sky with a nocturnal landscape. An inspired thought which evoked the mystery of a visible thing can be described by painting: indeed, it consists *uniquely* of visible things: skies, trees, people, solids, inscriptions, etc." [20]

The last sentence in this statement elucidates Magritte's intensely personal variant on a favorite surrealist device—the double image. He does not conceal one object or scene within another of different identity, as artists have done since the time of Arcimboldo and as picture-puzzle books customarily do. He portrays these objects and scenes as self-sufficient and crystal clear. And then he questions our capacity to believe by opposite factual statements, as when in the *Empire of Light, II* (page 50) we cannot be sure whether to turn on the street lights, contemplate the stars or, as seems much more likely, bask in the sun. It is part of Magritte's immense flexibility of imagination that he sometimes bewitches even himself, as when he misreads Manet's *Olympia* (see page 14) or cannot be positive whether he has painted a starry sky or one in

[20] René Magritte, letter to the writer, June 4, 1965. (Bibl. 25)

Hegel's Vacation. 1958. Oil, 23½ x 19¼". (Not in exhibition)

The Married Priest. 1961. Oil, 17¾ x 21¾. Collection Peter A. De Maerel, New York

which clouds float on a bright summer day. No question of naïveté is involved. The fact that he sometimes enchants himself as well as his audience is an integral part of his magic.

In *Golconda* (page 59) there is a downpour of those respectable figures in dark coats and derby hats which he often uses to challenge the conformity he pretends to illustrate. "*The Golden Legend*" (page 69) converts manna into zeppelins made of bread, and *Hegel's Vacation* (page 18) typifies Magritte's deliciously subversive wit in that an umbrella supports a tumbler full of the water it is meant to repel.

Magritte's preoccupation with a horseman as subject dates back many years. Indeed, according to Mesens, it was a theme which fascinated the artist soon after his mature career began, as when he painted a picture called *The Lost Jockey*.[21] The slow and apparently rather painful evolution of the image as it appears in *The Childhood of Icarus* (page 63) has been traced through its early stages by Magritte himself.[22] It remains, nevertheless, one of the most difficult of his iconographical motifs to follow with precision. We are on far surer ground in considering the picture called *The Soul of Bandits* (page 66) for which the preliminary drawings exist and have been kept together in the sequence here reproduced (pages 64, 65). The drawings are self-explanatory in so far as any traces of Magritte's unpredictable creative process can be. They require study rather than elucidation. The same thing might be said of Magritte's art as a whole. Since the solution of mystery remains one of the most irresistible of all human temptations, it is difficult not to yield to it. For example, one may find or invent a parallel between Magritte's image of a rifle stacked against a wall and his picture of a free-standing amputated human leg, conceivably part of the rifle's guilt in that it wears an Army boot (page 67). Or one may accept the painter's own conception of a recurrent theme in his art—a triparted nude woman (opposite) of which he has said, "that was just a dream about the present: each torso section represents a past generation." [23]

If the explanation seems far-fetched, it should be remembered that Magritte's art *is* far-fetched in both the literal and the figurative sense of the word, and deliberately so. This art comes from deep regions of the perceptive mind where only true artists, poets or musicians can breathe. Once surfaced, its equivocations remain inspired. It should be our startled purpose, not to probe but to respect and enjoy them.

Delusions of Grandeur. 1962. Oil, 39½ x 32″. Alexander Iolas Gallery. (Not in exhibition)

[21] E. L. T. Mesens, "René Magritte," *Peintres belges contemporains*, Brussels, 1947 (?)., p. 158. (Bibl. 57)

[22] "Lifeline," *op. cit.*, p. 22.

[23] *Time*, June 21, 1948.

1898
Nov. 21, René-François-Ghislain Magritte born at Lessines, a small town in the province of Hainaut in Belgium. A year later his family moves to nearby Gilly.

1910
The Magrittes go to live in Châtelet, where René and other local children study sketching. Magritte frequents the old cemetery at Soignies during summer vacations spent with relatives.

1913
Magritte, his father and two brothers settle in Charleroi, his mother having drowned in the Sambre River the year before. Meets his future wife, Georgette Berger.

1916–1918
Studies intermittently at the Academy of Fine Arts in Brussels. Receives a brochure on futurist art and thinks, half-seriously, of becoming an abstract painter. Magritte family settles permanently in Brussels in 1918.

1919
Magritte begins to associate with young painters, poets and musicians in Brussels.

1922
Marriage to Georgette. To earn a living, works as a designer of wall paper. Paints on his own, and experiments with Victor Servranckx in abstraction. Is shown a reproduction of Giorgio de Chirico's painting, *The Song of Love* (1914), which changes his conception of what painting *might* be.

1924
Allied with Camille Goemans, E. L. T. Mesens, Marcel Lecomte and, slightly later, Paul Nougé, in activity parallel to that of the Parisian surrealists. Contributes a statement to the Dada review, *391* (no. 19). Paints what he considers to be his first serious picture.

1925
Encouraged by the security of a contract with the new Galerie Le Centaure in Brussels, produces a large body of work, painting as many as sixty paintings in a year's time.

1927
Magritte's first one-man show at Galerie Le Centaure is unfavorably received by critics. In August he moves to a Paris suburb, Perreux-sur-Marne. Close association with the Parisian surrealists, especially André Breton and Paul Eluard.

1930
Somewhat weary of the polemical atmosphere in Parisian art circles, returns to Brussels where, except for occasional visits to France, Holland and England, he has lived ever since. Resumes old friendships with artists and writers in Brussels. Among new associates are Louis Scutenaire, Paul Colinet and Marcel Mariën.

1936
First one-man exhibition in America, Julien Levy Gallery, New York.

1930–1940
Represented in all important international exhibitions of surrealist art. Writes numerous articles and short statements elucidating his conception of art's potentials.

1940–1946
In spite of the grim austerity of living conditions in wartime Belgium, Magritte's palette takes on the brilliance of sunlight. For a period he borrows the technique of the impressionists, especially Renoir. Experiment badly received by both friends and detractors and finally abandoned.

Photograph by Shunk-Kender, Paris, 1965.

1948
For several months Magritte prepares for his forthcoming exhibition in Paris at the Galerie du Faubourg by reviving the audacious style of the French *fauves* of the early 20th century. The artist himself refers to this brief period as "*l'époque vache.*" Soon reverts to the precise and painstaking technique which was his heritage from the early Flemish masters.

1949
First exhibition at Alexander Iolas Gallery in New York, which has represented him there since, as well as in the Iolas galleries in Paris and Geneva.

1953
Commissioned by the Casino at Knokke-Le Zoute on the North Sea to design a series of eight themes for murals in the grand salon. The actual murals executed by Raymond Art and his assistants.

1957
Painting, *La Fée ignorante*, design for mural in the Palais des Beaux-Arts at Charleroi, executed under his supervision.

1960
First retrospective exhibition in the United States, Museum for Contemporary Arts, Dallas, Texas.

1961
Painting, *Les Barricades mystérieuses*, design for mural in the Palais des Congrès, Brussels, executed under his supervision.

Catalogues of major one-man exhibitions are listed in the bibliography on page 71. Magritte is represented in the following international exhibitions: Venice Biennale, 1948, 1954; Pittsburgh International, Carnegie Institute, 1950; Sao Paulo Bienal, 1957, 1965; Documenta II, Kassel, 1959.

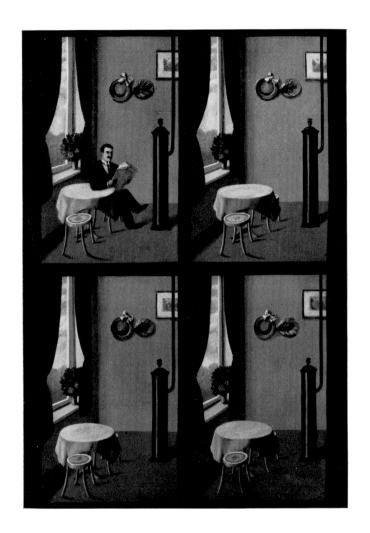

ABOVE: *Man with Newspaper.* 1927–28. Oil, 46 x 31½". Tate Gallery, London
ABOVE RIGHT: *The Spells of the Landscape.* c.1930. Oil, 21¼ x 28¾". Casino of Knokke, Belgium
RIGHT: *School is Out.* 1925? Oil, 29½ x 39⅜". Collection Ruth Spaak, Choisel, S/O, France

RIGHT: *The Empty Mask.* 1928. Oil, 32 x 45¾". Collection Mr. and Mrs. Raymond J. Braun, New York

BELOW RIGHT: *On the Threshold of Liberty.* 1929. Oil, 44⅞ x 57½". Collection J. Berthold Urvater, Brussels. (Not in exhibition)

BELOW LEFT: *The Bold Sleeper.* 1927. Oil, 43¼ x 33½". Collection Claude Spaak, Choisel, S/O, France

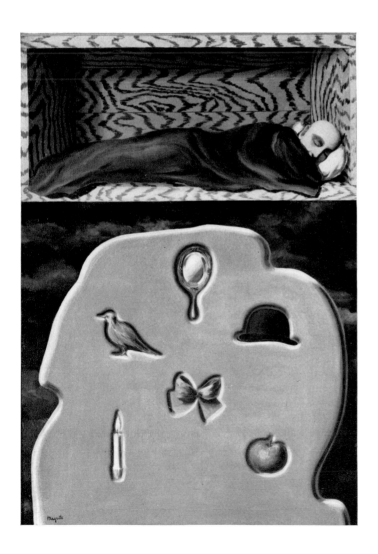

ABOVE: *The Key of Dreams*. 1930. Oil, 31⅞ x 23⅝". Private collection, Paris

ABOVE RIGHT: *The Palace of Curtains, III*. 1928–29. Oil, 32 x 44¾". Sidney Janis Gallery, New York

RIGHT: *The Wind and the Song*. 1928–29. Oil, 23¼ x 31½". William N. Copley Collection

ABOVE: *The False Mirror.* 1928. Oil, 21¼ x 31⅞". The Museum of Modern Art, New York. Purchase
BELOW: *Flowers of the Abyss, I.* 1928. Oil, 21½ x 28½". Collection Harry Torczyner, New York

ABOVE: *Threatening Weather*. 1928. Oil, 21½ x 28¾". Collection Roland Penrose, London
RIGHT: *The Ladder of Fire, I.* 1933. Oil, 21¼ x 28¾". Private collection, London

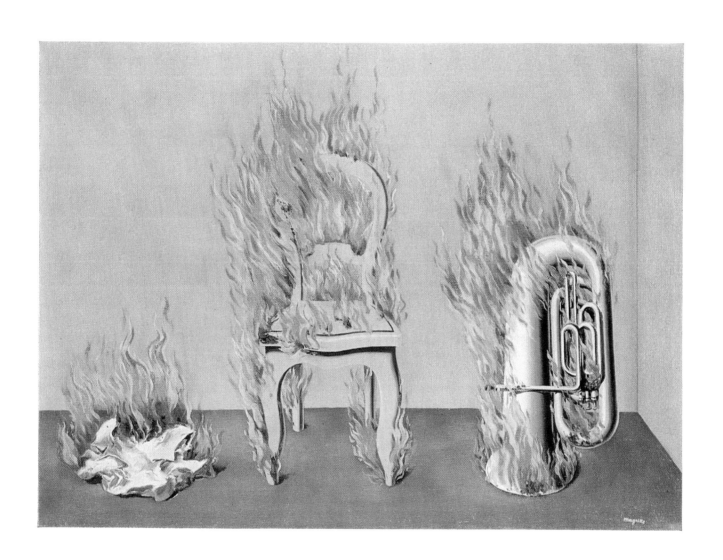

RIGHT: *Amorous Perspective*. 1935. Oil, 45¾ x 31⅞″. Collection Robert Giron, Brussels
BELOW: *The Collective Invention*. 1934. Oil, 31⅞ x 45¾″. Collection E. L. T. Mesens, London

The Voyager. 1935. Oil, 21¼ x 25⅝″. Collection Georges F. DeKnop, Brussels

RIGHT: *Perpetual Motion.* 1934. Oil, 21¼ x 28¾″. Grosvenor Gallery, London
BELOW: *The Annunciation.* 1929. Oil, 44⅞ x 57½″. Collection E. L. T. Mesens, London

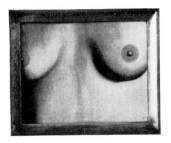

The Eternal Evidence. 1930. Oil; five panels, top to bottom, 8¼ x 4¾", 7⅝ x 9½", 10¾ x 7⅝", 8¾ x 6⅜", 8¾ x 4¾". William N. Copley Collection

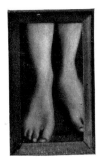

LEFT: *The Promenades of Euclid.* 1955. Oil, 63¾ x 51¼".
Alexander Iolas Gallery, New York, Paris, Geneva
RIGHT: *The Fair Captive, II.* 1935. Oil, 18 x 25½". Collection Robert Strauss, London
BELOW: *The Human Condition, I.* 1934. Oil, 39⅜ x 31½".
Collection Claude Spaak, Choisel, S/O, France

RIGHT: *In Praise of Dialectic.* 1937. Oil, 25⅝ x 21¼".
Collection Robert Giron, Brussels
BELOW: *Spontaneous Generation.* 1937. Oil, 21¼ x 28¾".
Collection Mme Jean Krebs, Brussels

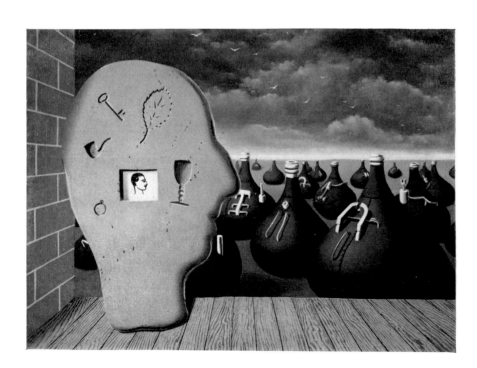

LEFT: *Time Transfixed.* 1939. Oil, 57¾ x 38½". Collection Edward James
BELOW: *Memory.* 1938. Oil, 29⅛ x 21¼". Collection Joachim Jean Aberbach, Sands Point, New York

RIGHT: *"Philosophy in the Boudoir."* 1947. Oil, 31⅛ x 24¼". Private collection
BELOW: *The Red Model.* 1935. Oil, 29 x 19¾". Moderna Museet, Stockholm

38

ABOVE: "*The Tomb of the Wrestlers.*" 1960. Oil, 35 x 46″. Collection Harry Torczyner, New York
RIGHT: *The Listening Chamber.* 1953. Oil, 31½ x 39⅜″. William N. Copley Collection

ABOVE: *The Therapeutic, II.* 1937. Oil, 35½ x 25½". Collection
J. Berthold Urvater, Brussels. (Not in exhibition)
RIGHT: *The Liberator.* 1947. Oil, 39 x 31". Los Angeles County
Museum of Art, gift of William N. Copley
LEFT: *The Alphabet of Revelations.* 1935. Oil, 21⅜ x 28⅞".
Private collection

LEFT: *The Rights of Man*. 1945. Oil, 57½ x 44⅞". Galleria del Naviglio, Milan
BELOW: *Elemental Cosmogony*. 1949. Oil, 31 x 39". Collection Christophe de Menil Thurman, New York

ABOVE: *Perspective: Madame Récamier of David*. 1951. Oil, 24¼ x 32⅛". Alexander Iolas Gallery, New York, Paris, Geneva
LEFT: *Perspective. The Balcony of Manet*. 1949. Oil, 31⅛ x 23". Collection Dr. Umberto Agnelli, Turin

LEFT: *Nostalgia*. 1941. Oil, 39⅜ x 31⅞″. Collection E. L. T. Mesens, London
BELOW: *Personal Values*. 1952. Oil, 32 x 40″. Collection J.-A. Goris, Brussels

LEFT: *Empire of Light, II.* 1950. Oil, 31 x 39″. The Museum of Modern Art, New York, gift of Dominique and John de Menil
BELOW: *The Banquet.* 1958. Oil, 38 x 50¾″. Collection Mr. and Mrs. Edwin A. Bergman, Chicago

LEFT: *Memory of a Voyage, III*. 1951. Oil, 33 x 25½".
Collection Adelaide de Menil, New York
ABOVE LEFT: *Memory of a Voyage*. 1955. Oil, 63⅞ x 51¼".
The Museum of Modern Art, New York, gift of Dominique
and John de Menil
ABOVE RIGHT: *Intimate Journal, I*. 1951. Oil, 31½ x 25¾".
Gallery Schwarz, Milan

"*The Castle of the Pyrenees.*" 1959. Oil, 78⅝ x 55⅛". Collection Harry Torczyner, New York

ABOVE: *The Glass Key*. 1959. Oil, 51 x 63½″. Collection D. and J. de Menil
LEFT: *The Song of Love*. 1948. Oil, 30½ x 39″. Collection Mr. and Mrs. Joseph R. Shapiro, Chicago

Ready-Made Bouquet. 1957. Oil, 62⅝ x 50⅝". Collection Mr. and Mrs. Barnet Hodes, Chicago

ABOVE: *Golconda*. 1953. Oil, 315⁄8 x 393⁄8″. Collection D. and J. de Menil
BELOW LEFT: *Pandora's Box*. 1951. Oil, 177⁄8 x 215⁄8″. Yale University Art Gallery, gift of Dr. and Mrs. John A. Cook, '32
BELOW RIGHT: *The Masterpiece or the Mysteries of the Horizon*. 1955. Oil, 191⁄2 x 251⁄2″. Alexander Iolas Gallery, New York, Paris, Geneva

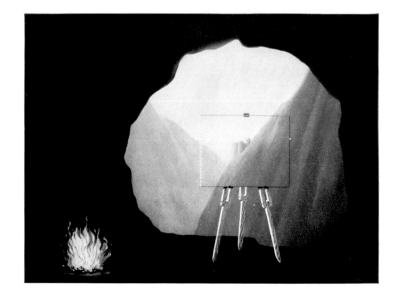

ABOVE: *The Companions of Fear*. 1942. Oil, 27⅝ x 36⅝″.
Collection Mme Jean Krebs, Brussels
RIGHT: *The Human Condition*. 1935. Oil, 21½ x 28¾″.
Collection Robert Strauss, London

ABOVE: *The Fanatics*. 1955. Oil, 23⅝ x 19¾". Casino of
Knokke, Belgium
RIGHT: *The Stated Place*. 1955. Oil, 32¼ x 23⅝". Collection
Mr. and Mrs. Edwin A. Bergman, Chicago. (Not in exhibi-
tion)

LEFT: *The Memoirs of a Saint*. 1960. Oil, 31½ x 39¼". Loan Collection, University of St. Thomas, Houston
BELOW: *The Difficult Passage*. 1964. Oil, 31⅞ x 39⅜". Alexander Iolas Gallery, New York, Paris, Geneva

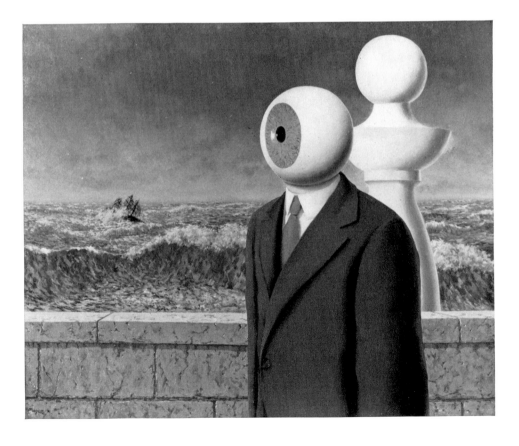

LEFT: *The Anger of the Gods*. 1960. Oil, 24 x 19¾″. Collection Joachim Jean Aberbach, Sands Point, New York
BELOW: *The Childhood of Icarus*. 1960. Oil, 38½ x 51″. Alexander Iolas Gallery, New York, Paris, Geneva

1re idée

" Lettres persanes "

et sa genèse, à Harry Torczyner
René Magritte 1960

I

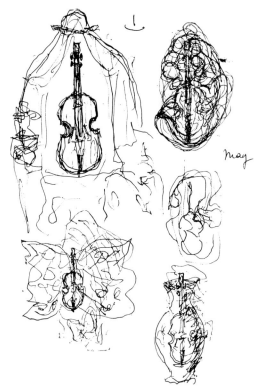

Mag

IV

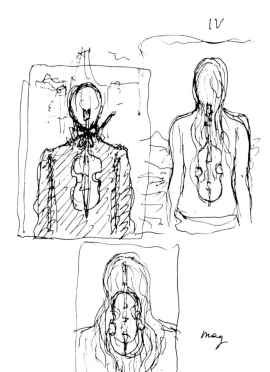

Mag

V

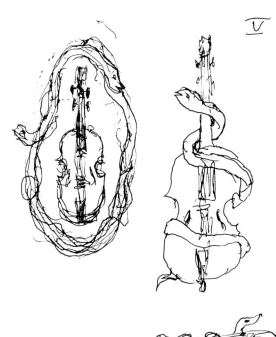

Mag

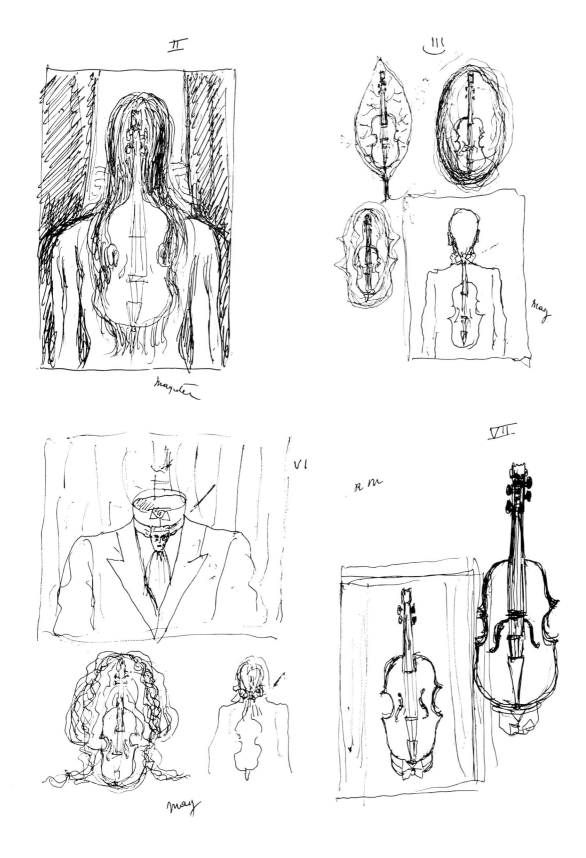

II

III

Magritte

May

VI

VII

xm

May

PRECEDING PAGE: *Persian Letters* (Lettres persanes). 1960. Collection Harry Torczyner, New York. (Not in exhibition). Pen and ink drawings for the painting *The Soul of Bandits*.

66

The Soul of Bandits. 1960. Oil, 25½ x 19¾″. Alexander Iolas Gallery, New York, Paris, Geneva. (This painting was originally entitled *Les Lettres persanes.*)

LEFT: *The Well of Truth*. 1963. Oil, 31⅞ x 23⅝″. Alexander Iolas Gallery, New York, Paris, Geneva

BELOW: *The Survivor*. 1950. Oil, 31⅛ x 23⅝″. William N. Copley Collection

68

ABOVE: *The Territory.* 1958. Oil, 28¾ x 45⅝". Collection Joachim Jean Aberbach, Sands Point, New York
BELOW RIGHT: *The Idol.* 1965. Oil, 21¼ x 25½". Alexander Iolas Gallery, New York, Paris, Geneva
BELOW LEFT: *The Labors of Alexander.* 1950. Oil, 23 x 19". Collection Brooks Jackson, New York

LEFT: *Blank Signature*. 1965. Oil, 31⅞ x 25½″. Alexander Iolas Gallery, New York, Paris, Geneva
BELOW: *"The Golden Legend."* 1958. Oil, 37½ x 50¾″. Collection Harry Torczyner, New York

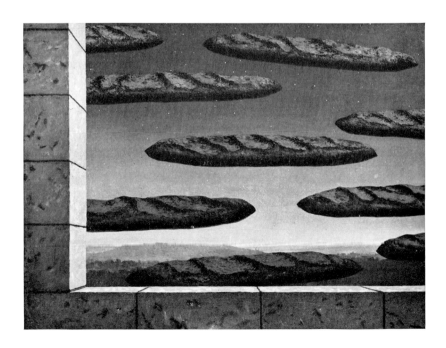

Portrait. 1961. Oil, 51¼ x 38¼". Private collection

This bibliography is a very selective one. The following categories have been excluded: references to newspaper articles, brief exhibition reviews which can be found through the Art Index, books and articles containing only reproductions of Magritte's work, books illustrated by him. Since Magritte is represented in all major surrealist exhibitions, and in practically every major general exhibition, only catalogues of his one-man shows have been included, limited to those accessible to the compiler. The listing of the writings by Magritte is by no means complete as many of the "small" and esoteric surrealist publications, to which he contributed, are now unobtainable.

All items in the bibliography, with one exception (bibl. 31), have been examined by the compiler. Those that are in the Museum Library have been marked with an asterisk (*). In case the Library has only a photocopy of a specific article it is marked with an (x).

In building up the Library's holdings of Magritte documentation I have had valuable assistance from Mr. André Blavier in Belgium, whose Magritte bibliography of 1960 (bibl. 121) also has been very useful.

Inga Forslund

WRITINGS AND STATEMENTS BY MAGRITTE
(arranged chronologically)

*1.   [Statements.] "391" no. 19:4, 1924.

x2.   Jusqu'où l'évolution peut mener. OEsophage no. 1, Mar. 1925.

       In the same number (only one published) "Urbanisme" by Magritte and "Les 5 commandements" by Magritte and E. L. T. Mesens.—Also a drawing by Magritte, made 1924.

*3.   Les mots et les images. La révolution surréaliste v. 5, no. 12:32–33 Dec. 15, 1929.

       English translation by E. L. T. Mesens in the catalogue of the exhibition "Magritte: Word vs image" at Sidney Janis Gallery, New York, 1954. (Bibl. *116.)

*4.   La poésie transfigurée. Par René Magritte, E. L. T. Mesens, Paul Nougé, André Souris. [3] p. Tract signed Jan. 1932.

       Reprinted in Nougé, Paul, Histoire de ne pas rire. Brussels, Les Lèvres nues, 1956, p. 92–95. (Bibl. *95.)

x5.   L'Action immédiate. Documents 34 (Brussels) n.s., no. 1, June 1934 (numéro spécial: "Intervention surréaliste"), p. 1–4.

       Signed by René Magritte, E. L. T. Mesens, Paul Nougé, Jean Scutenaire, André Souris.

Reprinted in Nougé, Paul, Histoire de ne pas rire. Brussels, Les Lèvres nues, 1956, p. 98–103. (Bibl. *95.)

x6.   Le fil d'Ariane. Documents 34 (Brussels) n.s., no. 1, June 1934 (numéro spécial: "Intervention surréaliste") p. 15.

       Reprinted in Cahiers d'art (Paris) v. 10, no. 5/6: 130, 1935. (*.)

x7.   Réponse du peintre René Magritte. Les Beaux-Arts (Brussels) no. 164:15, May 17, 1935.

       Answer to inquiry "Que pense-t-il de l'art 'officiel' de l'U. R. S. S. tel qu'il nous fut montré, l'été dernier, à la Biennale de Venise?"

*8.   Du temps que les surréalistes avaient raison. Paris, Éditions surréalistes, Aug. 1935. 15 p.

       Signed by Magritte, Breton, Dali, Dominguez, Eluard and others.

x9.   La ligne de vie. July 1938. 18 p.

       Manuscript of lecture given by Magritte at the Musée des Beaux-Arts in Antwerp, Nov. 20, 1938. Photocopy of original in the Museum of Modern Art Library.—Extracts printed in Combat (Brussels) v. 3, no. 105:5, Dec. 10, 1938. (x).—English translation "Lifeline" in View v. 7, no. 2:21–23, Dec. 1946. (x).

*10. L'Art bourgeois. Par René Magritte et Jean Scutenaire. London Bulletin no. 12:13–14, Mar. 15, 1939.

*11. Colour—colours or An experiment by Roland Penrose. By René Magritte and Paul Nougé. London Bulletin no. 17:9–12 incl. ill., June 15, 1939.

       Translated from the French by Iqbal Singh. Reprinted in the original "Une expérience de Roland Penrose" in Nougé, Paul, Histoire de ne pas rire. Brussels, Les Lèvres nues, 1956, p. 116–120. (Bibl. *95.)

*12. Le graduel de l'Eurëka. La feuille chargée (Jette-Brussels) Mar. 1950: [3–5].

*13. [Answer to inquiry:] Quel sens donnez-vous au mot poésie? La carte d'après nature (Brussels), special no., Jan. 1954:[25].

*14. La réconciliation. La carte d'après nature (Brussels) special no., Jan. 1954:[2].

*15. La pensée et les images. Arts plastiques (Brussels) special no., June 1954:39–43 incl. 2 ill.

       Reprint of Magritte's preface in catalogue of his exhibition at the Palais des Beaux-Arts in Brussels. (Bibl. *117.)

*16. Un art poétique. La carte d'après nature (Brussels) no. 8:[6] Jan. 1955.

       Reprinted in catalogue of Magritte exhibition at Galerie "Cahiers d'Art," Paris, Dec. 1955. (Bibl. *118.)

*17. La fin de l'octroi. [Par] Paul Colinet et René Magritte. *La carte d'après nature* (Brussels) no. 8:[8] Jan. 1955.

*18. La fée ignorante. *Bizarre* (Paris) no. 3:44 plus 2 ill. Dec. 1955.
[Statements.] 1957. To Mr. and Mrs. Barnet Hodes. *See bibl.* *33.

*19. A propos de "L'Univers du son." *Phantomas* (Brussels) v. 7, no. 15/16:26 Jan. 1960.

*20. L'Aveugle. [Poem.]—Le travail.—Le cochon. *Rhétorique* no. 2:[7–8], Aug. 1961.

*21. The art of resemblance.
Introduction to catalogue of Magritte exhibition at the Obelisk Gallery, London, 1961. (Bibl. *124). Also translated into Dutch "De kunst van de gelijkenis" by Hugo van de Perre in *Kroniek van kunst en kultuur* v. 21, no. 8:49–51, 1961. (*.)

*22. [Statement.] *Rhétorique* no. 5:[7], Apr. 1962.

* La poésie visible. *See bibl.* *128.

*23. [Interview.] *Arts* (Paris) no. 877:13, July 11–17, 1962. Interview by Marcel Fryns on the occasion of the Magritte exhibition at Knokke-Le Zoute.

*24. Leçon de choses. Ecrits et dessins. *Rhétorique* no. 7, Oct. 1962. 8 p.

x25. [Letter to James T. Soby.] June 4, 1965. [4] p. Photocopy of original in the Museum of Modern Art Library.—Also in English translation by Monroe Wheeler.
Also statements in the following exhibition catalogues: Bibl. *112, 119, *120, *122, *127, *129, *131, *132, *134, *135.

BOOKS ON MAGRITTE

*26. DEMARNE, PIERRE. René Magritte. Tilleur-lez-Liège, André Bosmans, 1961. [14] p. plus 24 pl. (Rhétorique no. 3, 1961.)
Extracts reprinted in catalogue of Magritte exhibition at Knokke-Le Zoute, 1962, p. 13 (Bibl. *128).

*27. Dix tableaux de Magritte, précédés de descriptions. Brussels, Le Miroir infidèle, 1946. [7] p. plus 10 pl.

*28. GOMEZ-CORREA, ENRIQUE. El espectro de René Magritte. Santiago de Chile, Ediciones Mandrágora, 1948. [34] p. incl. ill.
Poems to paintings by Magritte.—Edition of 500 numbered copies.

*29. MARIEN, MARCEL. Magritte. Préface par Marcel Mariën. Brussels, Les Auteurs associés, 1943. 14 p. plus 23 col. pl., port.

*30. NOUGE, PAUL. René Magritte ou Les images défendues. Dix-neuf reproductions de tableaux. Brussels, Les Auteurs associés, 1943. 65 p. incl. 19 ill.
Reprinted in Nougé, Paul, Histoire de ne pas rire. Brussels, Les Lèvres nues, 1956, p. 223–260 (with the addition "Des moyens et des fins" p. 255–256). This is the first complete text. (Bibl. *95).
Extracts of the text first published in *Le surréalisme au service de la révolution* no. 5, 1933:24–28. (*)

31. SCUTENAIRE, LOUIS. René Magritte. Brussels, Editions Librairie Sélection, 1947. 99 p. 13 pl.

*32. ———, ———. René Magritte. 2 éd. Edité par le Ministère de l'éducation nationale et de la culture. Brussels, 1964. 13 p. plus 25 ill. (1 col.), port. (Monographies de l'art belge.)
First edition published by De Sikkel, Antwerp, 1948.

*33. ———, ———. Magritte. Chicago, William and Noma Copley Foundation, [1962?] 17 p. incl. 3 ill. plus 7 pl. (1 col.).
Foreword by Joshua C. Taylor.—Text by Scutenaire, translated from the French by Eleanor Hodes.— Includes statements by Magritte, 1957, to Mr. and Mrs. Barnet Hodes.
Translation of Scutenaire's essay on Magritte published in 1948.

ARTICLES ON MAGRITTE

*34. ALLOWAY, LAWRENCE. Portrait of the artist no. 125. [René Magritte.] *Art News and Review* (London) v. 5, no. 21:1 Nov. 14, 1953.
On the occasion of the exhibition at Lefevre Gallery, London.

*35. BOSMANS, ANDRE. Montrer du doigt la connaissance. *Rhétorique* no. 2:[18–23] incl. ill., Aug. 1961.
Analyzes the following paintings by Magritte: "L'Etat de Grâce," "La Poitrine" and "La Présence d'Esprit," which also are reproduced.
———, ———. René Magritte ou la connaissance du monde. *See bibl.* 121.
BRETON, ANDRE. Envergure de René Magritte. *See bibl.* *135.

*36. BROCKWAY, FREDERICK. Sidelights on the Magritte exhibition. *London Bulletin* no. 2:18, 23 plus ill. May 1938.

*37. CALAS, NICOLAS. What is the real illusion? *Art News* v. 61, no. 4:33–34, 60–61 plus 2 col. ill. Summer 1962.

x38. CANADAY, JOHN. Floating rocks and flaming

tubas. *Horizon* v. 4, no. 3:76–82 plus 5 p. of ill. Jan. 1962.

> Reprinted in abbreviated form in Canaday's "Embattled Critic," N. Y., Farrar, Straus and Cudahy, 1962, p. 107–111, under the title "The delightful disconcerter: René Magritte." (*.)

* CARLUCCIO, LUIGI. [Introduction.] *See bibl.* *126.

*39. CHAR, RENÉ. La jeunesse illustrée. Titre d'un tableau de René Magritte. *Cahiers G.L.M.* (Paris) no. 6:52–53, Nov. 1937.

*40. COLINET, PAUL. "Le domaine enchanté." Panorama surréaliste de René Magritte. [1953]. [4] p.

> Poetic description of eight panels in the Casino at Knokke, published on the occasion of the inauguration.—Reprinted in bibl. *128.

* ———, ———. Pour se délivrer des explications. *See bibl.* *114.

*41. CONNOLLY, CYRIL. Surrealism. *Art News Annual* no. 21:133–162, 164, 166, 168, 170 incl. ill. (partly col.) Dec. 1951.

*42. CRISPOLTI, ENRICO. Brevi appunti per Magritte. *See bibl.* *132.

*43. ELUARD, PAUL. René Magritte. [Poem.] *In* his "Donner à voir," Paris, Gallimard, 1939. p. 198–199.

> Originally published in *Cahiers d'art* v. 10, no. 5/6:130, 1935, and in Eluard's "Les yeux fertiles," Paris, G.L.M., 1936.—Translated by Man Ray in *London Bulletin* no. 1:15, Apr. 1938 (*). Reprinted, together with Eluard's poem "A René Magritte" in his *Voir*, Geneva-Paris, Trois Collines, 1948, p. 76. (*.)
> Both poems frequently reprinted in exhibition catalogues.

*44. FIERENS, PAUL. Tradition du fantastique en Belgique. *Arts plastiques* (Brussels) special no., June 1954:5–20 incl. ill.

> Magritte p. 17, 18 plus 2 ill. p. 19, 20.

*45. GABLIK, SUZI. Meta-trompe-l'oeil. *Art News* v. 64, no. 1:47–48 incl. 3 ill. Mar. 1965.

x46. ———, ———. René Magritte: mystery painter. *Harper's Bazaar* v. 97, no. 3024:146–149, 190–191 incl. ill. Nov. 1963.

* ———, ———. See also bibl. *129.

*47. GOTTLIEB, CARLA. The pregnant woman, the flag, the eye: three new themes in twentieth century art. *Journal of Aesthetics and Art Criticism* v. 21, no. 2:177–187, Winter 1962.

> Magritte p. 184 (Analysis of his painting "The False Mirror.")

*48. GUASCO, RENZO. René Magritte. *D'Ars agency* (Milan) v. 6, no. 1:41–43 incl. 4 ill. (1 col.) Jan. 20/Apr. 20, 1965.

* HECKE, P. G. VAN. La peinture de René Magritte. *See bibl.* *102.

*49. ———, ———. René Magritte. *Le Centaure* (Brussels) v. 1, no. 7:131–133 incl. 1 ill. Apr. 1927.

> Reprinted in extended form in *Sélection*, 1927, and in somewhat abbreviated form in the catalogue of the Magritte exhibition at Knokke-Le Zoute, 1962 (Bibl. *128).

*50. JAGUER, EDOUARD. Au pays des images défendues. *Aujourd'hui* v. 5, no. 27:10–17, June 1960.

*51. JENNINGS, HUMPHREY. In Magritte's paintings . . . *London Bulletin* no. 1:15, Apr. 1938.

x52. JOUFFROY, ALAIN. Biographies des peintres: Magritte. *Jardin des arts* (Paris) no. 66 (special no.): 59, Apr. 1960.

*53. LECOMTE, MARCEL. La cascade. *Rhétorique* no. 5:[5], Apr. 1962.

> Commentary to Magritte's painting "La cascade," which also is reproduced in color.

* ———, ———. La lumière poétique. *See bibl.* *128.

*54. ———, ———. Quelques tableaux de Magritte et les textes qu'ils ont suscités. *Brussels. Musées Royaux des Beaux-Arts de Belgique. Bulletin.* 1964/1–2:101–110 incl. ill.

* LIBERO, LIBERO DE. René Magritte o il miraggio nel deserto. *See bibl.* *114.

* MAC AGY, DOUGLAS. About the art of Magritte. *See bibl.* *122.

*55. MESENS, E. L. T. Les apprentis magiciens au pays de la pléthore. *Arts plastiques* (Brussels) special no., June 1954:31–38 incl. ill.

> Magritte p. 33–35 incl. 2 ill.

x56. ———, ———. The cabinet of curiosities. The world of René Magritte. *The Saturday Book* no. 19:273–276 plus 8 p. of ill. (4 col.), 1959.

x57. ———, ———. René Magritte. *In* Peintres Belges Contemporains. Brussels, Editions Lumière, 1947? p. 157–161.

> Extracts reprinted in catalogue of Magritte exhibition at Knokke-Le Zoute, 1962. (Bibl. *128.)

* ———, ———. A self-appointed mission in contemporary art. *See bibl.* *123.

* NOUGE, PAUL. L'Avenir des statues! *See bibl.* *104.—Also included in *bibl.* *30.

* ———, ———. Avertissement.—Les grands voyages. *See bibl.* *103, *95.

* NOUGE, PAUL. Les circonstances de la peinture. *See bibl.* *102, *95.

* ———, ———. "Elémentaires." *See bibl.* *107, *95.

*58. ———, ———. Final advice to Humphrey Jennings. *London Bulletin* no. 1:5–6, Apr. 1938.
English translation by Humphrey Jennings of introduction "Dernières recommendations" in catalogue of Magritte exhibition in London 1938. Reprinted in bibl. *95.

x59. ———, ———. René Magritte ou La révélation objective. *Les Beaux-Arts* (Brussels) no. 203:18–19 incl. 7 ill. May 1, 1936.—Reprinted in bibl. *95.

*60. PERRE, HUGO VAN DE. René Magritte. *Kroniek van kunst en kultuur* v. 21, no. 8:52–60, 1961.

x61. R[AGGHIANTI, CARLO LUDOVICO]. Accoucheurs de flammes. *Critica d'arte* v. 1, no. 3:267–273 plus 9 ill., May 1954.

*62. RAPIN, MAURICE. Comme un seul homme. [1] p. Tract, Feb. 3, 1955.

*63. READ, HERBERT. Magritte. *London Bulletin* no. 1:2 plus 2 ill. Apr. 1938.

*64. REAVEY, GEORGE. "The endless chain." *London Bulletin* no. 2:23, May 1938.

x65. REICHARDT, JASIA. René Magritte. *Apollo* v. 75, no. 440:115 incl. 2 ill. Oct. 1961.

* SCUTENAIRE, JEAN. Trois fenêtres. *See bibl.* *106.

*66. SCUTENAIRE, LOUIS. En parlant un peu de Magritte. *Cahiers d'art* v. 30:255–264 incl. ill. plus 2 pl., 1955.

*67. ———, ———. Gloser à propos de l'exposition parisienne à Paris des oeuvres de René Magritte est prématuré. Allons-y donc! *Au miroir d'Elisabeth* (Brussels) May 1948.

*68. ———, ———. L'OEuvre peinte de René Magritte. *Savoir et beauté* (La Louvière) v. 41, no. 2/3:2415–2418 incl. ill., 1961.

* ———, ———. Les pieds dans le plat. *See bibl.* *111.

*69. ———, ———. René Magritte. *La terre n'est pas une vallée de larmes* (Brussels) 1945:38–47 plus 4 p. of ill.

* ———, ———. See also bibl. *113, 119, *128.

*70. SHELLEY, ROBERT. On a painting, "Le regard intérieur," by René Magritte. (A poem.) *Tiger's eye* no. 7:84–85 Mar. 15, 1949.

*71. TORCZYNER, HARRY. The magic of Magritte. *The Art Gallery* v. 7, no. 4:6–11 incl. ill. (partly col.) Jan. 1964.

* TYLER, PARKER. René Magritte. *See bibl.* *109.

*72. The vision of René Magritte. *Arts Magazine* v. 36, no. 10:14–15 incl. 3 ill. (2 col.) Sep. 1962.

*73. WALDBERG, PATRICK. René Magritte: l'inspiration et le mystère. *XXe siècle* n.s. v. 25, no. 22:10–18 incl. ill. (3 col. pl.) Dec. 1963.

* WERGIFOSSE, JACQUES. Commentaries. *See bibl.* *110.

* ———, ———. La joie de vivre. *See bibl.* *108.

GENERAL WORKS

*74. BRETON, ANDRE. Entretiens 1913–1952. Paris, Gallimard, 1952. p. 154, 162, 179, 221.

*75. ———, ———. Le surréalisme et la peinture suivi de Genèse et perspective artistique du surréalisme et de Fragments inédits. 2 ed. N. Y., Brentano's, 1945. p. 96.
English translation of "Genèse et perspective artistique du surréalisme" in bibl. *85.

*76. [———, ———, & ELUARD, PAUL.] Dictionnaire abrégé du surréalisme. Paris, Galerie Beaux-Arts, 1938. p. 16 plus ill. p. 52–53 and passim.

*77. BRION, MARCEL. Art fantastique. Paris, Albin Michel, 1961. passim plus 1 col. pl.

*78. COLLECTION URVATER. Brussels, Editions de la connaissance, 1957. n.p. ill. (partly col.) (Les grandes collections belges.)
Catalogue of collection shown during 1957 in the Museum Kröller-Müller, Otterlo and in the Musée des Beaux-Arts, Liège.—Introduction by Em. Langui.—Includes biographies.—9 works by Magritte (all reproduced, 1 in color).

*79. DICTIONARY OF MODERN PAINTING. General editors: Carlton Lake and Robert Maillard. 2 ed. N. Y., Tudor, 1964?
p. 212–213: Magritte by Claude Spaak. Translation of the French edition "Dictionnaire de la peinture moderne," Paris, Hazan.

80. FIERENS, PAUL. L'Art en Belgique, du moyen âge à nos jours. Brussels, Renaissance du Livre, 1947. p. 452, 530, 532, 533, 1 ill. p. 527.

*81. ———, ———. Le fantastique dans l'art flamand. Brussels, Editions du Cercle d'Art, 1947. p. 91–92 plus 1 pl.

*82. GAFFE, RENE. Peinture à travers dada et le surréalisme. Brussels, Editions des Artistes, 1952. p. 78–82 plus 1 ill.

*83. GASCOYNE, DAVID. A short survey of surrealism. London, Cobden-Sanderson, 1935. p. 84, 92, 105, 107, 108, 127.

*84. GENAILLE, ROBERT. La peinture en Belgique de Rubens aux surréalistes. Paris, Pierre Tisné, 1958. p. 143–147, 201; col. pl. p. 146.

*85. GUGGENHEIM, PEGGY, ed. Art of this century . . . 1910 to 1942. N. Y., Art of this century, 1942. p. 118.
Includes English translation of André Breton's "Genèse et perspective artistique du surréalisme" from bibl. *75.

*86. HAESAERTS, PAUL. Histoire de la peinture moderne en Flandre. Préface de Herman Teirlinck. Brussels, Les Editions de L'Arcade, 1960. p. 44, 207–220, 235, 236, 249–250 incl. 1 ill.

*87. HISTORY OF MODERN PAINTING. v. 3. From Picasso to Surrealism. Geneva, Skira, 1950. p. 150, 182.
Translation of the French edition "Histoire de la peinture moderne."—Also other language editions.

*88. JANIS, SIDNEY. Abstract & surrealist art in America. N. Y., Reynal & Hitchcock, 1944. p. 7, 86, 125.

*89. JEAN, MARCEL. The history of surrealist painting. By Marcel Jean with the collaboration of Arpad Mezei. N. Y., Grove Press, 1960. p. 177–187 and passim. ill.
Translation of the French edition "Histoire de la peinture surréaliste," Paris, Editions du Seuil, 1959.

*90. KYROU, ADO. Le surréalisme au cinéma. 2 éd. Paris, Le Terrain vague, 1963. p. 196, 198.
First edition 1953.

*91. LEGRAND, F[RANCINE] C[LAIRE]. La peinture en Belgique des primitives à nos jours. Brussels, Editions de la Connaissance, 1954. p. 58 plus pl. 95.

*92. LEVY, JULIEN. Surrealism. N. Y., The Black Sun Press, 1936. p. 19, 22, 31. ill. p. 144–145.

*93. NADEAU, MAURICE. The history of surrealism. N. Y., Macmillan, 1965. p. 22, 155, 156, 200, 1 ill.
Translation of the French edition "Histoire du surréalisme", first published in 2 volumes by Editions du Seuil, Paris, 1945 and 1948.

*94. NEW YORK. MUSEUM OF MODERN ART. Fantastic art, dada, surrealism. Edited by Alfred H. Barr, Jr. Essays by Georges Hugnet. 3d ed. N. Y., Museum of Modern Art, 1947, p. 47, 48 (in article "In the light of surrealism" by Georges Hugnet), p. 255–256 plus 3 ill.
First edition published 1936 as catalogue and text for an exhibition.—The article "In the light of surrealism" by Georges Hugnet reprinted in the Bulletin of the Museum of Modern Art, v. 4, no. 2–3, Nov.–Dec. 1936.

*95. NOUGE, PAUL. Histoire de ne pas rire. Brussels, Les Lèvres nues, 1956. 315 p.
The chapter "Magritte à travers tout le reste" includes: Lettre à René Magritte (1927).—Les images défendues (bibl. *30).—Rétrospective: Les circonstances de la peinture. René Magritte. Avertissement. Les grands voyages. Dernières recommandations. 1939. Grand air. Elémentaires. Les points sur les signes.—L'occasion et les sortilèges: L'aube désarmée. René Magritte ou la révélation objective.
All articles in "Rétrospective" were introductions to Magritte exhibitions, 1927–1948.

*96. RAYNAL, MAURICE. Modern painting. Geneva, Skira, 1953. p. 307–308 and ill. p. 256.
Translation of the French edition "Peinture moderne," 1953.

*97. SALKIN, ALEX. Modern painting in Belgium. 3 ed. N. Y., Belgian government information center, 1950. (Art, life and science in Belgium. 8.) p. 61–62, 64.

*98. SCHMELLER, ALFRED. Surrealism. N. Y., Crown, n.d. p. 8 and pl. 15 and 16 with commentaries p. 44 and 46.
Translation of the German edition, published as vol. 5 in the series Zeit und Farbe, ed. by Heinrich Neumayer, Vienna, Rosenbaum, 1956.

*99. SEUPHOR, M[ICHEL]. Un renouveau de la peinture en Belgique flamande. Paris, Les Tendances nouvelles, 1932. p. 97, ill. no. 3.
URVATER COLLECTION. See COLLECTION URVATER.

*100. WALDBERG, PATRICK. Surrealism. Lausanne, Skira, c.1962. (The taste of our time. 37) p. 78–83 and passim. ill. (col. pl.)
Translation of the French edition.

*101. WALRAVENS, JAN. Peinture contemporaine en Belgique. Antwerp, Editions Helios, 1961. p. 13–14 plus ill.

EXHIBITION CATALOGUES (arranged chronologically)

*102. LE CENTAURE, GALERIE, BRUSSELS. Exposition Magritte. [8] p. incl. 3 ill.
Apr. 23—May 3, 1927.—61 works.—Includes "La peinture de René Magritte" by P.-G. van Hecke [p. 3].—"Les circonstances de la peinture" by Paul Nougé [p. 5].

*103. GISO, SALLE, BRUSSELS. E. L. T. Mesens & E. van Tonderen présentent seize tableaux de

René Magritte. 14 p.

1931.—16 works.—Includes "Avertissement" (p. 5–11) and "Les grands voyages" (p. 13–14), both by Paul Nougé.

*104. BRUSSELS. PALAIS DES BEAUX-ARTS. Exposition René Magritte. [4] p.

May 27—June 7, 1933.—59 works.—Introduction "L'Avenir des statues" by Paul Nougé.

*105. LEVY, JULIEN, GALLERY, NEW YORK. René Magritte. 1 leaf.

Jan. 3–20, 1936.—22 works.—includes poem "René Magritte" by Paul Eluard (translated by Man Ray).

*106. BRUSSELS. PALAIS DES BEAUX-ARTS. E. L. T. Mesens présente trois peintres surréalistes: René Magritte, Man Ray, Yves Tanguy. [20] p. incl. ill.

Dec. 11–22, 1937.—12 works by Magritte.—Introduction by Jean Scutenaire: "Trois fenêtres" p. [1–2].—Also includes "Qu'est-ce que le surréalisme?" by André Breton, p. [3].—The poem "René Magritte" by Paul Eluard. p. [5].

*107. DIETRICH, GALERIE, BRUSSELS. Magritte. [16] p.

Nov. 30—Dec. 11, 1946.—23 works.—Includes "Elementaires" by Paul Nougé, p. 5–13.

*108. VERVIERS. SOCIETE ROYALE DES BEAUX-ARTS. Catalogue de l'exposition René Magritte. [4] p.

Jan. 19—Feb. 2, 1947.—21 works.—Introduction "La joie de vivre" by Jacques Wergifosse, p. [1–2].

*109. HUGO GALLERY, NEW YORK. René Magritte. [4] p.

Apr. 9—30, 1947.—45 works.—Includes "René Magritte" by Parker Tyler, p. [2–3].

*110. HUGO GALLERY, NEW YORK. Magritte. [8] p. incl. ill.

May 1948.—29 works.—Commentaries by Jacques Wergifosse (translated by Allan Ross).—Includes Paul Eluard's poem "A René Magritte."

*111. GALERIE DU FAUBOURG, PARIS. Magritte. Peintures et gouaches. [8] p.

May 11—June 5, 1948.—25 works.—Introduction "Les pieds dans le plat" by Louis Scutenaire, p. [3–5].

*112. COPLEY GALLERIES, BEVERLY HILLS. Magritte. [12] p. incl. ill.

Sept. 9, 1948.—29 works.—Includes short statement by Magritte (translated into English) and Paul Eluard's poem "A René Magritte" (in French).

*113. HUGO GALLERY, NEW YORK. Magritte. [4] p.

Mar. 20—Apr. 11, 1951.—39 works.—Includes "René Magritte" by Louis Scutenaire (translated into English by Waldemar Hansen).

*114. GALLERIA DELL'OBELISCO, ROME. René Magritte. [6] p.

Jan. 19–31, 1953.—28 works.—Includes "René Magritte o il miraggio nel deserto" by Libero de Libero.—"Pour se délivrer des explications" by Paul Colinet.

*115. LEFEVRE GALLERY, LONDON. René Magritte. [8] p. incl. 3 ill.

Nov. 1953.—17 works.—Includes biography and bibliography.

*116. JANIS, SIDNEY, GALLERY, NEW YORK. Magritte: Word vs image. [An exhibition of early paintings by Magritte in which the artist engages the word vs the image.] 1 leaf, folded into 22 p.

Mar. 1–20, 1954.—21 works.—Includes Magritte's "Word vs image" (translated from the French by E. L. T. Mesens).

*117. BRUSSELS. PALAIS DES BEAUX-ARTS. René Magritte. Brussels, Editions de la Connaissance, 1954. 38 p. incl. ill. (2 col.).

May 7—June 1, 1954.—93 works.—Includes "La pensée et les images" by René Magritte, p. 5–8.—"Esquisse autobiographique, p. 9–12.—"L'eau qui a coulé sous le pont" (short statements on Magritte by different authors, arranged chronologically), p. 13–16.—Bibliography, p. 17–18 and list of exhibitions, p. 19–20.

*118. GALERIE "CAHIERS D'ART," PARIS. Exposition de peintures & gouaches de René Magritte. [4] p.

Dec. 21, 1955—Jan. 31, 1956.—20 works.—Includes "Un art poétique" by René Magritte.

119. BRUSSELS. MUSEE D'IXELLES. Magritte. [8] p. plus 16 ill. (1 col.)

1959.—112 works.—Includes statement by Magritte in facs., p. 1.—Introduction by Scutenaire, p. 2–4.

*120. RIVE DROITE, GALERIE, PARIS. René Magritte. [4] p.

Feb. 16—Mar. 12, 1960.—22 works.—Includes statement by Magritte.

121. LIEGE. MUSEE DES BEAUX-ARTS. Exposition Magritte. 31 p. plus 12 ill.

Oct. 14—Nov. 10, 1960.—76 works.—Includes "René Magritte ou La connaissance du monde" by André Bosmans, p. 7–8.—Bibliography by André Blavier and André Bosmans, p. 17–31.

*122. DALLAS. MUSEUM FOR CONTEMPO-
RARY ARTS. René Magritte in America. [38] p.
incl. ill. port.

Dec. 8, 1960—Jan. 8, 1961.—82 works.—In-
cludes statement by Magritte (in French and
English) and biographical outline.—"About the
art of Magritte" by Douglas MacAgy.—
Also shown in Houston Museum of Fine Arts,
Feb. 1961.

*123. GROSVENOR GALLERY, LONDON. Ma-
gritte. 15 p. incl. ill.

Sept. 27—Oct. 24, 1961.—28 works.—Includes
"A self-appointed mission in contemporary art"
by E. L. T. Mesens, p. 4-5.

*124. OBELISK GALLERY, LONDON. Magritte
paintings, drawings, gouaches. 44 p. incl. ill.
Sept. 28—Oct. 27, 1961.—28 works.—Catalogue
compiled and edited by Philip M. Laski, includ-
ing bibliography and list of exhibitions.—Introduction by Magritte "The art of resemblance"
(in facs. and English translation).—Inserted:
"Appreciations of Magritte" by Jean Arp, André
Bosmans, Pierre Bourgeois and others.

*125. LANDRY, ALBERT, GALLERIES, NEW
YORK. René Magritte in New York. Private collections. [4] p.

Oct. 17—Nov. 4, 1961.—50 works.

*126. GALATEA, GALLERIA, TURIN. Magritte.
[12] p. incl. ill.

Feb. 2-26, 1962.—21 works.—Introduction by
Luigi Carluccio.

*127. IOLAS, ALEXANDER, GALLERY, NEW
YORK. René Magritte. Paintings—gouaches—
collages. 1960—1961—1962. [6] p. plus pl.

May 3-26, 1962.—23 works.—Includes statement by Magritte (in French and in English
translation by Suzi Gablik), p. 3.

*128. KNOKKE-LE ZOUTE-ALBERT PLAGE. CA-
SINO COMMUNAL. L'Oeuvre de René Ma-
gritte. Brussels, Editions de la Connaissance S.A.,
1962. 50 p. incl. ill. (some col.)

July—Aug. 1962.—104 works.—Includes "La
poésie visible" by René Magritte, p. 5.—Essays
on Magritte by P.-G. van Hecke, Louis Scutenaire, Paul Nougé, E. L. T. Mesens, Pierre
Demarne and Marcel Lecomte, p. 7-15.—"Esquisse auto-biographi[que]," p. 16-18.—"Le
domaine enchanté" by Paul Colinet, p. 49-50.

*129. MINNEAPOLIS. WALKER ART CENTER.
The vision of René Magritte. [32] p. incl. ill. (6
col.)

Sept. 16—Oct. 14, 1962.—92 works.—Introduction by Suzi Gablik.—Includes statement by

Magritte (in French facs. and in English translation).

*130. BODLEY GALLERY, NEW YORK. Magritte.
[4] p. plus 5 pl.

Oct. 8-27, 1962.—26 works.

*131. SCHWARZ, GALLERIA, MILAN. Magritte.
[18] p. incl. ill.

Dec. 6-31, 1962.—17 works.—Includes statement by Magritte (in Italian, French and English).

*132. L'ATTICO. ROME. Magritte. [16] p. incl. ill.
(2 col.)

Jan. 9, 1963.—18 works.—Includes "Brevi appunti per Magritte" by Enrico Crispolti.—Inserted: Statement by Magritte and list of works
exhibited.

*133. CHICAGO. THE RENAISSANCE SOCIETY
AT THE UNIVERSITY OF CHICAGO. Magritte. [4] p.

Mar. 1—Apr. 10, 1964.—21 works, from Chicago collections and New York galleries.

*134. HANOVER GALLERY, LONDON. René Ma-
gritte. [20] p. mostly ill.

May 14—July 10, 1964.—34 works.—Includes
statement by Magritte.

*135. LITTLE ROCK. ARKANSAS ART CENTER.
Magritte. [38] p. incl. ill.

May 15—June 30, 1964.—97 works.—Includes
"Envergure de René Magritte" by André Breton. Also in English translation "The breadth of
René Magritte" by W. G. Ryan.—Statements
by Magritte (in French and English), and a pen
drawing by the artist made especially for the
catalogue.

Exhibition prepared by the Art Department of
the University of St. Thomas, Houston, Texas.

*136. IOLAS, ALEXANDER, NEW YORK—PARIS
—GENEVA. Magritte. Le sens propre. [8] p. plus
7 pl. (1 col.)

Exhibition in New York Jan. 11—Feb. 6, 1965.
—Previously shown in Geneva and Paris.—38
works.—Includes "Envergure de René Magritte" by André Breton, and statement by
Magritte.

Inserted in the New York catalogue translation
into English of Magritte's statement and the
Breton article (reprinted from the catalogue of
the Magritte exhibition at Arkansas Art Center,
Little Rock.)

*137. NOTIZIE, TURIN. Magritte. 16 p. incl. ill. (3
col.), port.

Mar. 25—Apr. 25, 1965.—16 works.—Includes
biography and short bibliography.

138. GUSTAVE DE SMET.—RENE MAGRITTE.
     —EDGARD TYTGAT. (1946.) Produced and
     directed by R. Cocriamont.—16 mm. 22 min. In
     French.

139. LA LEÇON DE CHOSES OU MAGRITTE.
     (1960). Produced and directed by Luc de Heusch.
     Scenario by J. Delcorde and L. de Heusch. Com-
     mentary by Magritte. Music by C. Delièges.
     Photography by F. Geilfus and O. Tourjansky.—
     35 mm. 15 min. Color. In French.

140. RENE MAGRITTE—MIDDLE CLASS MA-
     GICIAN. (1965). Directed by Jonathan Miller
     for Monitor Film, BBC Television. Script by
     George Melly.—16 mm. 17 min. 22 sec. Black &
     white. In English.

LENDERS TO THE EXHIBITION

Joachim Jean Aberbach, Dr. Umberto Agnelli, Mr. and
Mrs. Edwin A. Bergman, Mr. and Mrs. Raymond J.
Braun, Mr. and Mrs. Rolf K. Bungeroth, William N.
Copley Collection, Georges F. DeKnop, Peter A. De
Maerel, Ruth Moskin Fineshriber, Robert Giron,
J.-A. Goris, Mr. and Mrs. Barnet Hodes, Brooks
Jackson, Edward James, Casino of Knokke, Belgium,
Mme Jean Krebs, Mme Claude Marcy, Adelaide de
Menil, D. and J. de Menil, George de Menil, E. L. T.
Mesens, Roland Penrose, Richard M. Scaife, Mr. and
Mrs. Joseph R. Shapiro, M. and Mme Claude Spaak,
Robert Strauss, Mr. and Mrs. Harry G. Sundheim, Jr.,
Christophe de Menil Thurman, Harry Torczyner.

Loan Collection, University of St. Thomas, Houston;
Tate Gallery, London; Los Angeles County Museum of
Art; Yale University Art Gallery, New Haven; The
Museum of Modern Art, New York; Moderna Museet,
Stockholm.

Alexander Iolas Gallery, New York, Paris, Geneva;
Sidney Janis Gallery, New York; Grosvenor Gallery,
London; Galleria del Naviglio, Milan; Gallery Schwarz,
Milan.

SCHEDULE OF THE EXHIBITION

The Museum of Modern Art, New York:
    December 15, 1965—February 27, 1966
Rose Art Museum, Brandeis University, Waltham,
Massachusetts:
    April 3—May 1, 1966
The Art Institute of Chicago:
    May 30—July 3, 1966
The Pasadena Art Museum:
    August 1—September 4, 1966
University Art Museum, University of California,
Berkeley:
    October 1—November 1, 1966

Dimensons are in inches, height preceding width. Illustrated works are indicated with an asterisk. Works
shown in New York only are marked (NY).

Titles taken from books are given with quotation
marks.

*1. School is Out. *La Sortie de l'Ecole*. 1925? Oil on can-
    vas, 29½ x 39⅜". Collection Ruth Spaak, Choisel,
    S/O, France. Ill. p. 22

*2. The Menaced Assassin. *L'Assassin menacé*. 1926.
    Oil on canvas, 59⅞ x 76⅞". Collection E. L. T.
    Mesens, London. Ill. p. 10

3. The Atlantid (The Reflection). *L'Atlantide (Le Re-
   flet)*. 1927. Oil on canvas, 39½ x 28½". Grosvenor
   Gallery, London

*4. The Bold Sleeper. *Le Dormeur téméraire*. 1927. Oil
    on canvas, 43¼ x 33½". Collection Claude Spaak,
    Choisel, S/O, France. Ill. p. 23

5. The Imprudent One. *L'Imprudent*. 1927. Oil on
   canvas, 39⅜ x 28⅞". Collection Mr. and Mrs.
   Harry G. Sundheim, Jr., Chicago

*6. Man with Newspaper. *L'Homme au Journal*.
    1927–28. Oil on canvas, 46 x 31½". Tate Gallery,
    London. Ill. p. 22

*7. The Empty Mask. *Le Masque vide*. 1928. Oil on
    canvas, 32 x 45¾". Collection Mr. and Mrs. Ray-
    mond J. Braun, New York. Ill. p. 23

*8. The False Mirror. *Le Faux Miroir*. 1928. Oil on
    canvas, 21¼ x 31⅞". The Museum of Modern
    Art, New York. Purchase. Ill. p. 25

*9. Flowers of the Abyss, I. *Les Fleurs de l'Abîme, I*.
    1928. Oil on canvas, 21½ x 28½". Collection
    Harry Torczyner, New York. Ill. p. 25

*10. Threatening Weather. *Le Temps menaçant*. 1928.
     Oil on canvas, 21½ x 28¾". Collection Roland
     Penrose, London. Ill. p. 26

*11. The Palace of Curtains, III. *Le Palais de Rideaux,
     III*. 1928–29. Oil on canvas, 32 x 44¾". Sidney
     Janis Gallery, New York. Ill. p. 24

*12. The Wind and the Song. *L'Air et la Chanson*.
     1928–29. Oil on canvas, 23¼ x 31½". William N.
     Copley Collection. Ill. p. 24

*13. The Annunciation. *L'Annonciation*. 1929. Oil on
     canvas, 44⅞ x 57½". Collection E. L. T. Mesens,
     London. Ill. p. 30

14. Surprises and the Ocean. *Les Surprises et l'Océan*.
    c.1929–30. Oil on canvas, 39 x 29". Collection
    Ruth Moskin Fineshriber, New York

*15. The Eternal Evidence. *L'Evidence éternelle*. 1930.
     Oil on canvas; five panels, top to bottom, 8¼ x
     4¾", 7⅝ x 9½", 10¾ x 7⅝", 8¾ x 6⅜", 8¾ x
     4¾". William N. Copley Collection. Ill. p. 32

16. The Lifeline. *La Ligne de Vie.* 1930. Oil on canvas, 28⅛ x 29⅝". Collection Harry Torczyner, New York

*17. Key of Dreams. *La Clef des Songes.* 1930. Oil, 31⅞ x 23⅝". Private collection, Paris. (NY). Ill. p. 24

*18. The Spells of the Landscape. *Les Charmes du Paysage.* c.1930. Oil on canvas, 21¼ x 28¾". Casino of Knokke, Belgium. Ill. p. 22

*19. The Ladder of Fire, I. *L'Echelle du Feu, I.* 1933. Oil on canvas, 21¼ x 28¾". Private collection London. Ill. p. 27

20. The Light of Coincidences. *La Lumière des Coïncidences.* 1933. Oil on canvas, 23⅝ x 28¾". Collection Mme Claude Marcy. Honfleur, France. (NY)

*21. The Collective Invention. *L'Invention collective.* 1934. Oil on canvas, 31⅞ x 45¾". Collection E. L. T. Mesens, London. Ill. p. 28

22. "Dangerous Acquaintances." "*Les Liaisons dangereuses.*" 1934. Oil on canvas, 28⅜ x 25¼". Collection Mme Claude Marcy. (NY)

*23. The Human Condition, I. *La Condition humaine, I.* 1934. Oil on canvas, 39⅜ x 31½". Collection Claude Spaak, Choisel, S/O, France. Ill. p. 35

*24. Perpetual Motion. *Le Mouvement perpétuel.* 1934. Oil on canvas, 21¼ x 28¾". Grosvenor Gallery, London. Ill. p. 31

25. Revolution. *La Révolution.* 1934. Oil on plywood, 25⅝ x 19¾". Collection Claude Spaak, Choisel, S/O, France

*26. The Alphabet of Revelations. *L'Alphabet des Révélations.* 1935. Oil on canvas, 21⅜ x 28⅞". Private collection. Ill. p. 42

*27. Amorous Perspective. *La Perspective amoureuse.* 1935. Oil on canvas, 45¾ x 31⅞". Collection Robert Giron, Brussels. Ill. p. 28

*28. The Fair Captive, II. *La Belle Captive, II.* 1935. Oil on canvas, 18 x 25½". Collection Robert Strauss, London. (NY). Ill. p. 35

*29. The Human Condition. *La Condition humaine.* 1935. Oil on canvas, 21½ x 28¾". Collection Robert Strauss, London. (NY). Ill. p. 60

*30. The Frontiers of Summer. *Les Marches de l'Eté.* 1935. Oil on canvas, 23⅝ x 28¾". Collection Claude Spaak, Choisel, S/O, France. Ill. p. 33

*31. Portrait. *Le Portrait.* 1935. Oil on canvas, 28⅞ x 19⅞". The Museum of Modern Art, New York, gift of Kay Sage Tanguy. Ill. p. 2

*32. The Red Model. *Le Modèle rouge.* 1935. Oil on canvas, 29 x 19¾". Moderna Museet, Stockholm. (NY). Ill. p. 38

*33. The Voyager. *Le Voyageur.* 1935. Oil on canvas, 21¼ x 25⅝". Collection Georges F. DeKnop, Brussels. Ill. p. 29

*34. In Praise of Dialectic. *L'Eloge de la Dialectique.* 1937. Oil on canvas, 25⅝ x 21¼". Collection Robert Giron, Brussels. Ill. p. 36

35. The Song of the Storm. *Le Chant de l'Orage.* 1937. Oil on canvas, 25⅝ x 21⅜". Collection George de Menil, Houston, Texas

*36. Spontaneous Generation. *La Génération spontanée.* 1937. Oil on canvas, 21¼ x 28¾". Collection Mme Jean Krebs, Brussels. Ill. p. 36

*37. Memory. *La Mémoire.* 1938. Oil on canvas, 29⅛ x 21¼". Collection Joachim Jean Aberbach, Sands Point, New York. Ill. p. 37

*38. Time Transfixed. *La Durée poignardée.* 1939. Oil on canvas, 57¾ x 38½". Collection Edward James. Ill. p. 37

*39. Nostalgia. *Le Mal du Pays.* 1941. Oil on canvas, 39⅜ x 31⅞". Collection E. L. T. Mesens, London. Ill. p. 48

*40. The Companions of Fear. *Les Compagnons de la Peur.* 1942. Oil on canvas, 27⅝ x 36⅝". Collection Mme Jean Krebs, Brussels. Ill. p. 60

*41. The Rights of Man. *Les Droits de l'Homme.* 1945. Oil on canvas, 57½ x 44⅞". Galleria del Naviglio, Milan. Ill. p. 44

42. The Fair Captive. *La Belle Captive.* 1947. Oil on canvas, 20¾ x 25". Collection Brooks Jackson, New York

*43. The Liberator. *Le Libérateur.* 1947. Oil on canvas, 39 x 31". Los Angeles County Museum of Art, gift of William N. Copley. Ill. p. 43

44. The Red Model. *Le Modèle rouge.* 1947. Gouache, 18 x 14½". Alexander Iolas Gallery, New York, Paris, Geneva.

*45. "Philosophy in the Boudoir." "*La Philosophie dans le Boudoir.*" 1947. Oil on canvas, 31⅛ x 24¼". Private collection. Ill. p. 39

*46. The Song of Love. *Le Chant d'Amour.* 1948. Oil on canvas, 30½ x 39". Collection Mr. and Mrs. Joseph R. Shapiro, Chicago. Ill. p. 56

*47. Perspective: The Balcony of Manet. *Perspective: Le Balcon de Manet.* 1949. Oil on canvas, 31⅛ x 23". Collection Dr. Umberto Agnelli, Turin. (NY). Ill. p. 46.

*48. Elemental Cosmogony. *Cosmogonie élémentaire.* 1949. Oil on canvas, 31 x 39". Collection Christophe de Menil Thurman, New York. Ill. p. 45

49. Weights and Measures. *Les Poids et les Mesures.* 1949. Oil on canvas, 21¼ x 18¼". Collection Mr. and Mrs. Rolf K. Bungeroth, Pittsburgh, Pa. (NY)

*50. Empire of Light, II. *L'Empire des Lumières, II.* 1950. Oil on canvas, 31 x 39". The Museum of

Modern Art, New York, gift of Dominique and John de Menil. Ill. p. 50

*51. The Labors of Alexander. *Les Travaux d'Alexandre.* 1950. Oil on canvas, 23 x 19″. Collection Brooks Jackson, New York. Ill. p. 68

*52. The Survivor. *Le Survivant.* 1950. Oil on canvas, 31⅛ x 23⅝″. William N. Copley Collection. Ill. p. 67

*53. Intimate Journal, I. *Journal intime, I.* 1951. Oil on canvas, 31½ x 25¾″. Gallery Schwarz, Milan. Ill. p. 53

*54. Memory of a Voyage, III. *Souvenir de Voyage, III.* 1951. Oil on canvas, 33 x 25½″. Collection Adelaide de Menil, New York. Ill. p. 52

*55. Pandora's Box. *La Boîte de Pandore.* 1951. Oil on canvas, 17⅞ x 21⅝″. Yale University Art Gallery, gift of Dr. and Mrs. John A. Cook, '32. Ill. p. 59

*56. Perspective: Madame Récamier of David. *Perspective: Madame Récamier de David.* 1951. Oil on canvas, 24¼ x 32⅛″. Alexander Iolas Gallery, New York, Paris, Geneva. Ill. p. 47

*57. Personal Values. *Les Valeurs personnelles.* 1952. Oil on canvas, 32 x 40″. Collection J.-A. Goris, Brussels. Ill. p. 49

*58. Golconda. 1953. Oil on canvas, 31⅝ x 39⅜″. Collection D. and J. de Menil. Ill. p. 59

*59. The Listening Chamber. *La Chambre d'écoute.* 1953. Oil on canvas, 31½ x 39⅜″. William N. Copley Collection. Ill. p. 41

*60. The Invisible World. *Le Monde invisible.* 1953–54. Oil on canvas, 76⅞ x 51½″. Private collection. Ill. p. 54

*61. The Fanatics. *Les Fanatiques.* 1955. Oil on canvas, 23⅝ x 19¾″. Casino of Knokke, Belgium. Ill. p. 61

*62. The Masterpiece or the Mysteries of the Horizon. *Le Chef-d'œuvre ou les Mystères de l'Horizon.* 1955. Oil on canvas, 19½ x 25½″. Alexander Iolas Gallery, New York, Paris, Geneva. Ill. p. 59

*63. Memory of a Voyage. *Souvenir de Voyage.* 1955. Oil on canvas, 63⅞ x 51¼″. The Museum of Modern Art, New York, gift of Dominique and John de Menil. Ill. p. 53

*64. The Promenades of Euclid. *Les Promenades d'Euclide.* 1955. Oil on canvas, 63¾ x 51¼″. Alexander Iolas Gallery, New York, Paris, Geneva. Ill. p. 34

*65. Ready-Made Bouquet. *Le Bouquet tout fait.* 1957. Oil on canvas, 62⅝ x 50⅝″. Collection Mr. and Mrs. Barnet Hodes, Chicago. Ill. p. 58

*66. The Banquet. *Le Banquet.* 1958. Oil on canvas, 38 x 50¾″. Collection Mr. and Mrs. Edwin A. Bergman, Chicago. Ill. p. 51

*67. "The Golden Legend." "*La Légende dorée.*" 1958. Oil on canvas, 37½ x 50¾″. Collection Harry Torczyner, New York. Ill. p. 69

*68. The Territory. *Le Territoire.* 1958. Oil on canvas, 28¾ x 45⅝″. Collection Joachim Jean Aberbach, Sands Point, New York. Ill. p. 68

*69. "The Castle of the Pyrenees." "*Le Château des Pyrénées.*" 1959. Oil on canvas, 78⅝ x 55⅛″. Collection Harry Torczyner, New York. (NY). Ill. p. 55

*70. The Glass Key. *La Clef de Verre.* 1959. Oil on canvas, 51 x 63½″. Collection D. and J. de Menil. Ill. p. 57

*71. The Anger of the Gods. *La Colère des Dieux.* 1960. Oil on canvas, 24 x 19¾″. Collection Joachim Jean Aberbach, Sands Point, New York. Ill. p. 63

72. The Bosom. *La Poitrine.* 1960. Oil on canvas, 20 x 27½″. Collection Richard M. Scaife, Pittsburgh.

*73. The Childhood of Icarus. *L'Enfance d'Icare.* 1960. Oil on canvas, 38½ x 51″. Alexander Iolas Gallery, New York, Paris, Geneva. Ill. p. 63

*74. The Memoirs of a Saint. *Les Mémoires d'un Saint.* 1960. Oil on canvas, 31½ x 39¼″. Loan Collection, University of St. Thomas, Houston, Texas. Ill. p. 62

*75. The Soul of Bandits. *Un Peu de L'Ame des Bandits.* 1960. Oil on canvas, 25½ x 19¾″. Alexander Iolas Gallery, New York, Paris, Geneva. Ill. p. 66

*76. "The Tomb of the Wrestlers." "*Le Tombeau des Lutteurs.*" 1960. Oil on canvas, 35 x 46″. Collection Harry Torczyner, New York. Ill. p. 40

*77. The Married Priest. *Le Prêtre marié.* 1961. Oil on canvas, 17¾ x 21¾″. Collection Peter A. De Maerel, New York. Ill. p. 18

*78. Portrait. *Le Portrait.* 1961. Oil on canvas, 51¼ x 38¼″. Private collection. Ill. p. 70

*79. The Well of Truth. *Le Puits de Vérité.* 1963. Oil on canvas, 31⅞ x 23⅝″. Alexander Iolas Gallery, New York, Paris, Geneva. Ill. p. 67

*80. The Difficult Passage. *La Traversée difficile.* 1964. Oil on canvas, 31⅞ x 39⅜″. Alexander Iolas Gallery, New York, Paris, Geneva. Ill. p. 62

*81. The Idol. *L'Idole.* 1965. Oil on canvas, 21¼ x 25½″. Alexander Iolas Gallery, New York, Paris, Geneva. Ill. p. 68

*82. Blank Signature. *Le Blanc-seing.* 1965. Oil on canvas, 31⅞ x 25½″. Alexander Iolas Gallery, New York, Paris, Geneva. Ill. p. 69

Cover Photograph by Duane Michals, 1965